98-96

By the same author

SIGNS MAKE SENSE: A Guide to British Sign Language

HUMAN HORIZONS SERIES

SIGN IN SIGHT

A Step into the Deaf World

CATH SMITH

Illustrated by David Hodgson

A CONDOR BOOK
SOUVENIR PRESS (E&A) LTD

Reprinted 1995, 1996

First published 1992 by Souvenir Press (Educational & Academic) Ltd,
43 Great Russell Street, London WC1B 3PA
and simultaneously in Canada

ISBN 0 285 65100 5

Photoset and printed in Great Britain by
Redwood Books, Trowbridge, Wiltshire.

FOREWORD

I was very pleased to be asked to write a brief word of introduction to *Sign in Sight: A Step into the Deaf World*. I am myself a profoundly Deaf person and member of the Deaf Community, who was born into a hearing family. I hope that today's parents of deaf children will read this book to gain some insight into our Deaf World.

Being an avid reader of all books relating to 'Deaf Issues', I find this book very well balanced, without being too heavy. It covers many of the issues relative to the Deaf Community in sufficient detail to make it comfortable to read and understand.

I am quite sure that all those who have links with Deaf people will find *Sign in Sight* a very pleasant and informative book.

David Walker
North East Regional Officer,
The Royal National Institute for Deaf People

ACKNOWLEDGEMENTS

My sincere thanks to all the people who helped at various stages in the preparation of this book:

To David Hodgson whose skilful illustrations have helped to put Sign in sight.

To the people who read and gave comments on the first draft of the book, for their time, trouble and encouragement:

Judith Collins, Teaching Fellow, Deaf Studies Research Unit, Durham University.
Kathy Robinson, Writer and Teacher, Cleveland.
Granville Tate, Teacher, Durham.
David Walker, Royal National Institute for Deaf People, North East Regional Officer.

To the people who gave and checked information on the sections relevant to their work:

Dr Terry Morris, Headmaster, Beverley School for the Deaf, Middlesbrough.
David Thompson, Sound Advantage, subsidiary of the Royal National Institute for Deaf People.
Tricia Harris, Information Division, Royal National Institute for Deaf People.
Lynn Jackson, Information Division, Royal National Institute for Deaf People.
Trish Topping, TYPE TALK, National Telephone Relay Service (RNID).
Charles Donaldson, Editor, 'No Need to Shout', BBC Ceefax.
Charles Herd, Editor, 'Earshot', Channel 4 Oracle.
Austin Reeves, Honorary Secretary, Deaf Broadcasting Council.
Richard Gray, Controlling Manager, British Association of the Hard of Hearing.
A. Clark Denmark, Director of Education and Training Services, British Deaf Association.
Bernard Quinn, Director of Information Services, British Deaf Association.
Colin Redman, Information and Access Officer, National Deaf Children's Society.
Robert Ashby, Membership and Public Services Officer, National Deaf Children's Society.
Gary Taylor, Member of Deaf Accord.
Rikki Kittel, Membership Secretary and Treasurer, LASER.
Juliet Harlen, Information Assistant, SENSE.
Dr Mary Brennan, Co-director of Advanced Diploma and MA Courses in Sign Language Studies, Durham University.
David Brien, Co-director of Advanced Diploma and MA Courses in Sign Language Studies, Durham University.
Muriel Raine, Secretary, Deaf Studies Research Unit, Durham University.

T. Stewart Simpson, Chief Executive, Council for the Advancement of
Communication with Deaf People.

Ruth Roberts, Development Officer, Council for the Advancement of
Communication with Deaf People.

A very special thank you to:

My husband David and son William.

Steven Goodman, for typing and retyping drafts of the book, and finally, to the
Cleveland Deaf Community and the pupils of Beverley School for the Deaf.

CONTENTS

11

INTRODUCTION

Growing numbers of people are interested in learning more about the world of deafness and its language. Whether this interest springs from a desire to learn sign language or from a wish to find out more about the cultural aspects of deafness, the two are inextricably linked to such an extent that one cannot be viewed without reference to the other.

By presenting signs and text side by side it is hoped that this book will be not only more visually interesting, but also able to offer a fascinating insight into the experience of deafness, illustrating how signs can reflect Deaf people's way of thinking. Shared knowledge of the things that interest and influence Deaf people is vital to the learning of the language, since these are the things likely to be discussed. Such information, covered in this book, is the culmination of a Deaf and hearing working partnership and is intended to inspire those who read it to want to find out more from Deaf people, and to share in the Deaf experience.

Sign in Sight is primarily concerned with this 'Deaf World', the world of Britain's Deaf Community together with its culture and language, British Sign Language (BSL). In addition, it covers matters relevant to all deaf people and their families, particularly the parents of deaf children, and should provide essential knowledge and information to all students of sign language.

Few things can challenge our basic assumptions about language, values and society as can the Deaf world; it is an amazing world that not only exists, but thrives, often unseen, in the midst of hearing society. For those of us who are not Deaf, the cultural beliefs and language that we have grown up with are so much part of our being that it is almost impossible to imagine a world, culture and language so different from our own. We even rely on our spoken language to think about and discuss a culture and language of an entirely different nature, based on very different experiences and requiring a different way of thinking. However, even if deafness is outside our own personal experience, the desire to learn Deaf people's language ultimately reflects interest in and respect for Deaf people themselves, opening up new possibilities of sharing each other's language and culture.

Access to the Deaf community is by no means easy or straightforward for hearing learners, but is crucial to the learning of BSL and to give parents in particular the inspiration they will need. It is generally accepted that use of BSL is a prerequisite for membership of or access to the Deaf community; yet, paradoxically, regular interaction with Deaf people is essential if one is to acquire this language in the first place. *Sign in Sight* endeavours to link some of the facets involved, providing an introduction, an invitation to step into the world of deafness, that offers an increased awareness and wider perspective on the predicament of being Deaf in a hearing world — not as a tragedy, but as a unique difference.

GUIDE TO DRAWINGS

Sign vocabulary is only one aspect of a complex language system which is structured quite differently from spoken English. Sign language is highly inflectional and exploits space and movement in its grammatical processes, factors that need to be seen in use. The illustrations shown throughout this book are of sign vocabulary relevant to the topics being considered and are intended to *reinforce the interactive use of sign language* such as may be acquired in BSL classes taught by trained Deaf tutors.

There is as yet no written form of sign language in the accepted sense, although various complex notation systems have been developed for research purposes. In the written medium, such as this, it is convenient to use individual signs to illustrate some of the language features and help to reinforce some of the visual concepts. However, it must be explained that this can be misleading, as it tends to concentrate the mind on single sign units, out of context and uninflected, giving a simplistic view of a language as complex as any other.

Section Three focuses on BSL and the vocabulary presented is in a boxed style, with a heading (or gloss) above and caption below to describe particular details of hand shape and movement. This is for convenience of identification and discussion, and should not be regarded as the sign's sole meaning in every case.

In addition, although approximately 80 per cent of the signs of BSL can be considered standard throughout the country, 20 per cent are variable in a way that is comparable to accent and dialect in spoken language. Signs can also vary due to personal choice and preference, reflecting the style of different individuals, and some will vary enormously in different contexts. Like all living languages, BSL represents continuity tempered by *constant change*, and not all of the signs recorded here will remain the same indefinitely. It is advisable to check such changes and variations within your local Deaf community.

All other sections have sign drawings in a free style, unglossed and without captions. They all illustrate a word or concept on the *same page* of text on which they appear, usually in the order in which they are mentioned, and are highlighted in the text in bold type. These are not necessarily direct translations, but represent the closest meaning of each sign in the context in which it appears.

ARROWS

The following types of arrows mean:

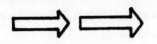

A broken movement.

Movement in one direction then the other.

Repeated movement.

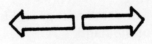

Hands move apart.

The sign ends with stress.

Hand or fingers open then close.

Open hand closes.

Closed hand opens.

Impact on point drawn.

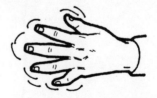

Very small repeated movements.

Hands drawn in dotted lines show the **start** of the sign. Hands drawn in solid lines show the **finish**.

Signs that are mimed actions of holding objects may have the object drawn in dotted lines to help people understand and remember them.

15

GUIDE TO CAPTIONS

In the captioned drawings in Section Three, signs and finger spelling are described and drawn as if the person making them is right-handed. Naturally, left-handed people will sign and finger-spell using the left hand as the dominant hand.

The captions are intended to add extra information to explain the movement of the hands which cannot always be shown in a drawing. Where possible, a full description of the sign is given, but in some cases the hand shapes may not be given if they are clear from the drawing.

To avoid misunderstandings and lengthy descriptions, set terms are used to describe:
1 Parts of the hand.
2 Common hand shapes.
3 Directions.

PARTS OF THE HAND

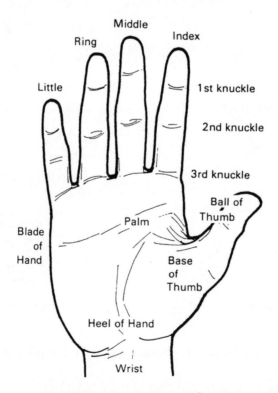

The right hand is always written as R.
The left hand is always written as L.

BASIC HAND SHAPES

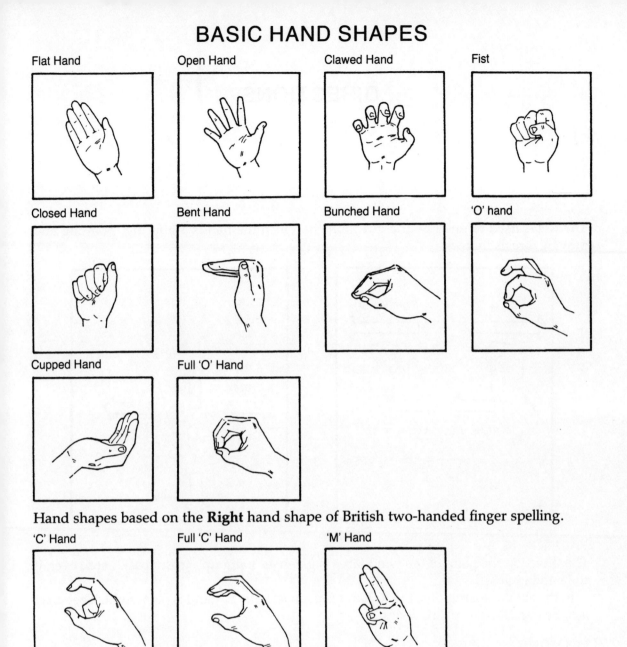

Flat Hand

Open Hand

Clawed Hand

Fist

Closed Hand

Bent Hand

Bunched Hand

'O' hand

Cupped Hand

Full 'O' Hand

Hand shapes based on the **Right** hand shape of British two-handed finger spelling.

'C' Hand

Full 'C' Hand

'M' Hand

'N' Hand

'R' Hand

'V' Hand

These are the most common hand shapes, but do not cover every shape used in signing. They may be further clarified, e.g. R. hand loosely cupped, L. hand slightly bent, two 'V' hands, fingers bent, etc.

If the caption says, e.g. index, middle finger and thumb extended, then it is understood that the other fingers are closed.

DIRECTIONS

The terms used to describe the directions in which the hands are facing, pointing and moving, are as follows:

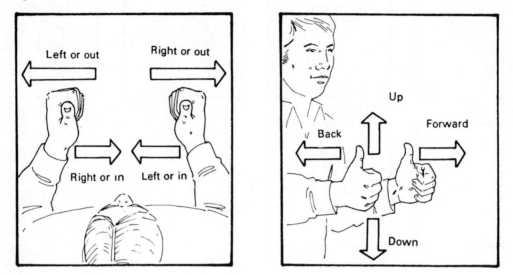

FACING
The direction the palm of the hand faces is given as 'palm up', 'palm back', etc., even if the hand is closed.

In the above illustrations, the R. hand is palm left, the L. hand is palm right. They may also be described as palms facing.

POINTING
The hand may be described as 'pointing' up, forward, etc., even if the fingers are bent in a different direction, or closed.

In the above illustrations, both hands are pointing forward, thumbs up.

MOVEMENT
Where a movement or position is diagonal, it is described as 'forward/left', 'back/right', etc.

Many movements are described as 'hands move **alternately**'. This means that they move at the same time in opposite directions as in 'up and down', or continuously in the same circular direction, alternately.

Some signs need a full description of hand shapes and positions before any movement is made. This is then called a **formation**. This means they keep their position together as they move.

Section One

DEAFNESS: LANGUAGE AND CULTURAL IDENTITY

LANGUAGE AND IDENTITY

Deafness is an all-embracing term that means different things to different people. It can occur at any age, and may vary in degree from slight to severe or total. The onset of deafness may be sudden or gradual, and may be linked to other conditions such as vertigo, tinnitus or visual impairment. Deafness may be caused by illness, injury or hereditary factors and may or may not be treatable — the effects can be as varied and individual as we are ourselves. However, it is useful to try and identify two broad and separate groups of deaf individuals for whom the effects of deafness are fundamentally different in terms of identity and communication. The implications of deafness from birth or infancy are different from those of deafness occurring later, the most crucial factor being language and cultural identity.

Our ability to communicate with others is one of the most valuable and significant features of our lives, and the means to communicate are based on a language that is acquired through dialogue and interaction with others. We may rarely stop to consider our own language development, as most of us acquired it in a seemingly effortless way years ago, before we can even remember. As adults, we can see the process being repeated: children are exposed to their mother tongue and gradually absorb it, using it to explore and learn about the world around them.

For most of us this process occurs through our ability to hear and interact with the spoken language that surrounds us, a process that is well established by the time we are of school age, ready to receive our formal education, through that language. If we were to lose our hearing after this early language development, through which our identity as a hearing person is established, we would still have the memory of sound and, more importantly, our thought processes and internal language, or 'inner voice', would be spoken language. We would have a 'hearing' mind even if we were never to hear again.

THE DEAFENED AND HARD OF HEARING MAJORITY

The majority of people with a hearing loss in this country, an estimated 7,500,000 people, have lost all or part of their hearing after spoken language and a hearing identity have been established in this way.

The onset of deafness can be devastating and traumatic, requiring support and re-habilitation, particularly in the area of communication. However, it is very likely that most deafened and hard of hearing people will retain English as their first language, and will continue to share the hearing cultural identity of the rest of society, forming a quite separate group from the Deaf linguistic and cultural minority.

THE DEAF CULTURAL AND LINGUISTIC MINORITY

Within the large number of deaf people mentioned above, there is a minority group whose culture and first language are not shared by the majority. For ease of identification throughout this book, the convention of the upper case 'D' in *Deaf* is used to distinguish members of this linguistic and cultural minority from deaf people whose primary identity is with hearing society. The lower case deaf is also used when referring to the audiological condition of not hearing and to refer to deaf children, since it is not clear at what point deaf children might adopt the conventions of the culture and become Deaf.

An estimated 50,000 people identify themselves as members of Britain's Deaf Community, bound together by common experiences, particularly early childhood deafness, and sharing a common language, BSL, Britain's fourth indigenous language after English, Welsh and Scots Gaelic. Deaf people live and work in the hearing world and regard the knowledge and use of English as both essential and valued in contacts with hearing people. However, most regard BSL as their dominant or preferred language, an important part of the separate cultural identity, shared by community members, that is barely comprehended by mainstream society.

The singular effects of early childhood deafness on language and communication are not readily seen or understood, and yet it is this factor, common within the community, that largely determines the linguistic and cultural development of its members.

One child in every thousand is born severely or profoundly deaf (or becomes so before the age of two); vision is likely to be their main link with the world and their main channel of communication, requiring access to a fluently used visual language. The paradox is that over 90 per cent of such children are not born into the Deaf community, among people like themselves who use visual language; they are born to hearing parents who have probably never encountered deafness before.

It is virtually impossible for those of us not born deaf, parents included, to imagine thought processes and language development in an entirely different medium. We think of language in terms of spoken words, because that is what language means to us. The very idea that language can develop independently of speech may never occur to us.

However, language can and does develop without access to spoken language. Sign languages flourish all over the world, wherever groups of Deaf people come together. All true sign languages that have been studied share common features of spatial grammatical structures that bear no relation to the spoken languages surrounding them. Each language has its own unique sign vocabulary and structural rules, but all are the creation of Deaf minds, having evolved through the national Deaf communities who use them. It would seem that, all over the world, Deaf people, tuned as they are to the visual channel, not only need but are able to generate visual language.

Sign languages do for Deaf people what spoken languages do for hearing people. Language gives meaning to the world around us, provides a vehicle for our thoughts, allows the development of complex and abstract concepts and enables us to recall and to relate events to others. The very essence of language is the communication it gives us with others who share our language. Since BSL is not shared by the majority, and is not usually the language of the home, at least initially, this puts deaf children and their families in a very unusual position.

DEAF CHILDREN IN DEAF FAMILIES

Language and culture are usually passed down from one generation to the next. Deaf children with Deaf parents in signing homes are likely to develop BSL as a first language (as are the hearing children of Deaf parents) and English as a *second language*. The child's first language and its associated culture are shared by the Deaf community and the child's own family. Research has shown that Deaf mothers with babies have a way of playing with movement and space in a visual way (hearing mothers tend to play more with speech and sound) and that this helps to lay the foundations for language through the visual channel, particularly eye contact and attention, so that the process of language acquisition can start in babyhood and proceed along much the same path as hearing language development.

DEAF CHILDREN IN HEARING FAMILIES

The situation in hearing homes is somewhat different. The language, culture and expectations will be that of hearing society. Deafness may not even be suspected until speech fails to develop, with diagnosis coming as a traumatic shock to many families. It is this failure to develop speech that often causes the greatest distress to parents, so natural does it seem to want our children to be like us. In these early days, parents need all the help they can get, from other parents and Deaf people as well as professionals.

Few deaf children have no experience of sound, but of all the sounds that deafness may preclude, speech is the most significant since, even with good amplification, the spoken language of the home and environment may not be heard at all. The foundations for language in either the auditory or the visual mode are likely to be delayed at least until deafness has been confirmed and in language terms much precious time will have already been lost, compared to hearing children and deaf children in signing homes. Unless specific steps are taken to give deaf children access to language in the mode they can *most easily acquire*, their disadvantage will become greater with each passing day, so rapidly do young children develop language in the pre-school years.

The ability to predict the possible future identity and development of all deaf children is very difficult indeed, but degree of deafness and age of onset remain powerful indicators of the possible future achievements in spoken language. This means that unless deaf children have some degree of hearing for speech purposes, or become deaf after early spoken language development, it is unlikely that English, the language of the home and society, will be their first natural language.

THE LANGUAGE OF EDUCATION

Except in the case of Deaf children in Deaf families, the early decisions regarding communication and education for the deaf child are almost invariably made by hearing people. Apart from a few isolated exceptions, the overwhelming reaction is to attempt to promote the language of the majority, both as the child's first language and as the language through which education is delivered. This is either in the form of exclusively 'oral/aural' methods, concentrating on speech and lip-reading to the total exclusion of sign language, or in various forms of sign systems used simultaneously with spoken English, which lack the visual integrity of sign language so vital to deaf children's early language development. The people who *are* comfortable with visual language, and who understand what it is like to be a deaf child in a hearing world, are rarely consulted.

THE LANGUAGE OF DEAF SCHOOL LEAVERS

The fact that English is not the first natural language for most profoundly deaf children has been borne out by a study carried out in 1979. It was found that most deaf school leavers had not progressed beyond a reading age of 8.75 years. In real terms, this means that they would be unable to read the tabloid newspapers, and that instruction manuals, government or official forms, safety regulations, and so on, would all remain beyond comprehension. In addition, speech quality was found to be largely unintelligible, and skill at lip-reading was found to be no better than inexperienced hearing children, dispelling the myth that deaf people are good lip-readers.

At the time of the study, deaf schools were almost exclusively oral. It is estimated that between 50 and 60 per cent of special schools now use a Total Communication approach, which embraces a wide range of communication methods including signs to support spoken English, but which rarely includes BSL. It is felt that Total Communication has improved education standards generally, but there is no evidence as yet to indicate any change in these specific English language skills. Deaf school leavers remain without a full share in the English language of the hearing majority in either its written or spoken form, even after more than ten years of hard and often dedicated tuition in full-time special education geared to teaching that language.

THE LANGUAGE OF THE SCHOOLS

Other studies have shown that most deaf school leavers *do* develop skill in BSL by the time they leave school. In most schools for the deaf, even where teachers do not sign, or use only English-based signed systems, there is a recognisable form of BSL used by the children. Although some vocabulary items may be specific to the school, school leavers quickly adapt to adult signing and claim to have learnt this before leaving school. So the shared language of the Deaf community, even if developed later than usual for a first language, does appear to become the dominant language for deaf children and one that is not only greatly needed, but also highly valued.

The need for, and ability to generate a visual language is clearly a powerful force in view of the fact that few hearing families have had contact with adult Deaf signers while their children were small. Many deaf children do not start to develop sign language until they have regular contact with others, and this is usually when they start school, providing it is a school with other deaf signing children. This can be as late as five years of age, already past what is considered to be the optimum time for language and cognitive development. In some parts of the country deaf children are integrated into hearing schools and may be denied access to sign language until even later, when they might opt to join the Deaf community from their own choice.

CHANGING ATTITUDES

Thankfully, attitudes to BSL and Deaf people's own potential are gradually changing. A number of important advances that have influenced change have been made in Britain over the past ten to fifteen years, and are described in Section Seven. More parents are now learning BSL and starting to seek early contact for their children with adult Deaf signers, thus providing access to visual language and the adult role models essential for the development of a positive Deaf identity. This also enables families to gain insight and access to the Deaf community through which they can gain support and understanding; they will then be able to offer their children a bicultural as well as a bilingual option.

However, the responsibility for learning BSL is not confined to the parents and families of deaf children, for whom it is essential in establishing the close and loving relationship that all children need. BSL also needs widespread acceptance and understanding within hearing society if young Deaf people are to be given opportunities equal to those available to hearing youngsters, and are to develop a positive self-image and self-esteem. By gaining confidence in themselves and their own abilities, they will be able to step into the hearing world with dignity.

TERMS AND SIGNS: CULTURAL DEAFNESS

It is interesting to look at some of the terms in current use, reflecting society's way of defining deafness, and also at the way they might be expressed in BSL, reflecting Deaf people's own cultural perspective.

The term 'pre-lingual' deafness is used when referring to deafness occurring at birth or in early childhood, and is used mainly by hearing professionals, but rarely by Deaf people themselves. The term means quite literally 'before language' and provides a useful distinction between early childhood deafness and deafness acquired later in life.

Deaf people who were born deaf, or who became so before language development, frequently identify themselves as **'born deaf'**, as in the top illustration, or as **'profoundly deaf'**, as in the illustration opposite, or as simply 'deaf', using the sign shown in all three illustrations.

Degree of deafness can be described as profound, severe or partial, although Deaf people mainly use 'profoundly deaf' to indicate a community member who prefers to communicate in BSL, and **'partially deaf'**, as in the last illustration, to indicate someone who has the option of communicating in speech, regardless of the actual degree of deafness.

TERMS AND SIGNS: ACQUIRED DEAFNESS

Deaf people's cultural perspective can again be seen in the terms and signs used to identify deafness occurring later in life.

The term 'post-lingual' deafness is used by some professionals to refer to individuals who are born hearing, and whose hearing loss occurs after spoken language is established. The term means 'after language' development, and, like 'pre-lingual', is rarely used by Deaf people, or by those who are deafened and hard of hearing.

There are several other terms used to refer to deafness occurring in adult life, or later in childhood. These include 'acquired deafness' or 'adventitious deafness'. In BSL these terms are often indicated by the concept **'become deaf'**, as in the illustration opposite, although the term and sign 'deafened', shown at the top of the page, is becoming increasingly used, and is also used to indicate **'hearing loss'** or 'deafness' in general terms.

Although some people make the distinction between 'deafened' and **'hard of hearing'** to indicate degree of hearing loss, either might be used as a blanket term to distinguish those losing their hearing in adult life from those born deaf.

COMMUNICATION MODES

INTRODUCTION

The communication systems referred to in this section are those in use amongst deaf people and do not specifically refer to methods used in the education of deaf children.

The effects of deafness on language development, as explained in Section One, partly determine the communication methods available to deaf people. However, since communication is two-way, at least in the sense that there is a sender and a receiver, a new set of variables comes into play when considering the language and communication abilities of others.

Deaf people live simultaneously in two worlds, a majority and minority culture, each having not only a different language base, but also a different medium in which to communicate. Although interest in learning BSL is spreading rapidly in the hearing community, most hearing people remain unfamiliar with sign language. For this reason both Deaf and deafened people may make use of a range and combination of methods to suit different people and different situations. For example, when at work or out shopping, a young Deaf person may communicate orally out of necessity, but use BSL when with Deaf friends. Similarly, a deafened adult may choose to learn BSL or SSE (Sign Supported English) to be able to participate in signed interpretation at conferences, or to join in group discussion, but prefer to communicate orally in a more relaxed one-to-one situation.

Not all modes of communication are effective for all individuals in all situations. In practice, both sides tend to adjust to the needs of a particular situation, concentrating on the transmission of the message through whatever codes or channels they can mutually use.

The essential options available are between the two communication modes of speech and sign, and between the two languages of English and BSL. These can be combined in a variety of ways which can be grouped into three general categories — spoken English, speech and sign combinations, and British Sign Language.

One possible way of viewing this is as a continuum between the two distinct languages, with English at one end and BSL at the other. Between these two languages there is a variety of language mixtures, which combine BSL and English in varying degrees.

People may vary in their use of language combinations along such a continuum, either as their preferred communication mode, or to accommodate the needs of other people, but *very* few deaf or hearing people are truly bilingual, able to function fully in both languages. Generally speaking, Deaf people are likely to function mostly at the BSL end of the continuum, and deafened and hearing people at the English end, with the possibility that neither party may fully share the language of the other. However, it is possible that as improved teaching methods and research into BSL have greater impact, and more deaf children have access to BSL as a first language, bilingualism is more likely to flourish.

ENGLISH-INFLUENCED VARIETIES OF BSL

Spoken English	Sign Supported English	Pidgin Sign English	Pidgin Sign Language	British Sign Language

ORAL COMMUNICATION: SPEECH AND LIP-READING

To start at the English end of the continuum, for people who are not able to hear speech (or who hear only part of it) the elements that remain are the **visual patterns of the mouth** in receiving information (lip-reading), and in producing speech for expression. It is generally accepted that even under the best circumstances, and for people whose first language is English, lip-reading is a very difficult task. Many speech sounds are invisible on the lips, and those that can be seen may look identical to others. Although a small number of deaf people are excellent lip-readers, most are not, and rely heavily on context or guesswork to distinguish meaning.

For Deaf people whose English may be a very poor second language, for the reasons described in Section One, this task is even more restricted, since lip-reading as a code for receiving spoken language cannot exceed the level of competence in that language — in other words, you can't lip-read the words of a language you don't fully understand.

The speech abilities of deafened people rarely cause a communication breakdown, but for Deaf people, as discussed on p. 24, speech intelligibility may be very limited, and some Deaf people prefer to use lip-patterns only, without voice, thus requiring the other party to lip-read them. However, in spite of the limitations, Deaf people do not avoid contact with hearing people, even though they acknowledge communication problems, and in everyday contact with hearing people such communication is primarily through speech and lip-reading.

LANGUAGE MIXTURES: SIGN SUPPORTED ENGLISH

Still at the English end of the continuum but adding signs to the picture, is the general category sometimes termed **Sign Supported English** (SSE). As its name suggests, *SSE is not a sign language* but a spoken language, that is, English (either voiced or unvoiced) combined with signs from the vocabulary of BSL, together with finger spelling.

It is important to clarify this point since many hearing people confuse SSE with BSL, because signs are involved, and attempt to use SSE in all situations with all deaf people. The term can also be used to describe a variety of BSL which is strongly influenced by English.

Since BSL is a separate language which is visually constructed, it is not possible for it to be matched simultaneously with spoken or mouthed English because the structures are completely different. The combination of speech and signs represents a contrived system rather than a language in its own right, but more importantly, it depends on a shared knowledge of English by those using it. Although a useful system for deaf people whose first language is English, or who are bilingual, SSE is largely inaccessible to many Deaf people, since it follows English word order and structures and can lead to the use of signs in different contexts which may either be meaningless or look absurd to BSL users.

LANGUAGE MIXTURES: SIGN PIDGINS

Within the Sign Supported English category, terms such as 'combined method' and 'simultaneous communication' may also sometimes occur to describe the fact that more than one language is being **mixed**, using two mediums at the same time.

When hearing and Deaf people come together, two languages meet and influence each other. It has been recognised that, in practice, a relatively stable contact language has developed between Deaf and hearing people. In the study of spoken languages, the term **'pidgin'** is used to describe languages containing a partial mix of two (or more) languages, but whose overall structure belongs fully to neither. This term is also sometimes used to describe English-influenced varieties of BSL.

In the English to BSL continuum, it is possible that there are two forms of pidgin. Nearer to English is a variety that can be termed Pidgin Sign English, containing a combination of predominantly English mouth patterns and word order, but including incorporation of some, or switches into full, BSL structures. Nearer to BSL, Pidgin Sign Language follows the grammatical structure of BSL, but might incorporate English mouth patterns to some degree, or include some switches into English.

These BSL/English pidgins possibly represent the most commonly used signed communication between Deaf and hearing people in current use, but, as stated in the Introduction, true bilingualism may become more prevalent with the increased recognition of BSL.

BRITISH SIGN LANGUAGE

Moving on from language mixtures that combine English and sign language in varying degrees, we reach the end of the continuum and the distinct language of BSL, **British Sign Language**.

The use of BSL is considered one of the chief identifying features of membership of Britain's Deaf Community, and is used extensively by members to communicate with other Deaf people, and with hearing people who know the language. Most Deaf people regard BSL as their primary language.

The hearing people most likely to be fluent signers are children of Deaf parents, and other family members who have grown up in signing environments. It is possible for professionals such as social workers and interpreters, and other hearing people who are not native signers, to develop skill in BSL as a second language.

VISUAL COMMUNICATION: OPTIMUM CONDITIONS

Bearing in mind that deafness cuts off or restricts communication through the auditory channel, consideration needs to be given to providing the best conditions for the visual reception of speech, or signs, whatever the language base or communication mode chosen.

Good visibility in well lit conditions is fundamental if communication is to be received visually with a minimum of eye strain. **Lighting on the face** of the 'sender' is particularly important, as information from the whole face is vital to the reception of both lip-reading and sign language.

Visual distractions need to be minimised, and for lip-readers, the distance between the parties should not be too great. It is easier to read speech and BSL if **both parties are facing each other** at a reasonable distance, and of course, **eye contact** is essential before exchanges can begin.

Section Three

BRITISH SIGN LANGUAGE

INTRODUCTION

Just as the effects of early profound deafness, described in Section One, can be difficult at first to appreciate, so the idea of a language based entirely on visual integrity can be an elusive concept to grasp. Sign is not merely a different language; it takes place in a different medium. This medium, of gestures organised in space, incorporating movement of the hands, face and body and which is perceived by the eyes, uses form and structure of an entirely different nature, but perfectly suited to a visual language.

It is not that this fact in itself is difficult to grasp, but in practice it is difficult to view such a language without using assumptions based on our experience of spoken language, and to look for familiar structures. When we think in terms of grammar, we inevitably think of structures used in spoken language, and look for them in BSL. English makes use of additional elements at the beginnings and endings of words, or includes extra words to describe and qualify information. This tends not to happen in BSL; it is far more likely that the movement of a sign will be changed in some way. Sometimes the movement changes its location or direction, or perhaps the movement is repeated slowly or rapidly, in a characteristic way that changes the sign's meaning.

In sign language, things or ideas can exist simultaneously in space, a factor not possible in spoken English and so quite unexpected to hearing people. Our understanding of language is based on words that are spoken, or written, and follow each other in sequence, but a visual language needs to be looked at quite differently. Different language media, for example the spoken or written forms of a language, bring their own restrictions. A gestural system involves certain motor constraints in sign production and visual constraints in sign perception, that can be compensated for in very unique ways.

Studies in America have shown that sign production is slower than word production by about half, and yet the proposition rate remains the same in both modes. This means that twice the number of words may be needed to express the same ideas that can be produced by signs in the same space of time. This is made possible by the way sign language is able to compress complex meaning into the signs themselves, by using such devices as changes in the movement, direction and placement, together with non-manual information carried by the face, eyes and body. These particular processes make it possible to produce ideas in a sign language such as BSL at the same rate as in a spoken language, even though the number of signs used is less than half the number of words, and this is a crucial factor.

Dictionaries and lexicons of sign languages tend to contain a small number of signs compared to the number of words in spoken language dictionaries, but this can be very misleading. Signs presented in such books tend to be in their citation form, that is in isolation and uninflected, like most of the ones in this book. The processes mentioned above, of compacting information, which can change and add meaning in an infinite number of ways, are rarely represented, partly because the study of sign languages is still very much in its infancy, but also because of the restrictions of presenting a moving visual language in a static printed medium. Many of these features, though crucial to the language, remain outside the scope of this book.

Sign language needs to be seen and used with Deaf people to be fully appreciated. However, many interesting facets of BSL can still be elicited from its vocabulary, as the brief glimpses in this section will hopefully show. These include some of BSL's special features, such as iconicity (visual imagery), classifying hand shapes and directional verbs, in addition to factors common to all languages, such as influences and borrowings from other languages.

ICONICITY (direct)

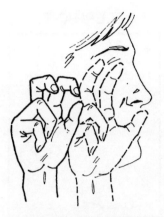

Iconicity is the term used to describe the pictorial element in sign language and comes from the Greek word 'icon', meaning 'image' or 'figure'. Although many signs may originate in a clearly iconic form, research has shown that over time signs tend to become more arbitrary, and their original visual links to meaning may become submerged.

The signs illustrated here give a very clear visual representation of the objects that they refer to. These examples depict various objects in their entirety and can be described as directly iconic.

Iconicity is present in all sign languages, but not necessarily in the same form. The BSL sign **tree**, for example, is the same in American Sign Language, but a different iconic version (not shown) is used in Danish Sign Language.

TREE

Right elbow cradled in L. hand; R. open hand, slightly clawed, twists from side to side.

BUTTERFLY

Palm back flat hands, locked at thumbs, make flapping movement.

TEAPOT

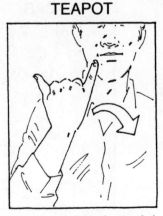

Little finger and thumb extended, hand tips in pouring action.

AEROPLANE

Little finger and thumb extended, hand moves forward near head.

ICONICITY (indirect)

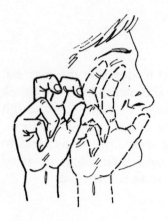

BIRD

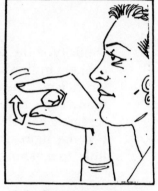

Index finger and thumb open and close in front of mouth like a beak.

ELEPHANT

Full handed 'C' moves down/forward from face to indicate trunk.

RABBIT

Palm forward 'N' hands bend several time at sides of head to indicate ears.

FLOWER

Bunched hand twists from side to side under nose in action of smelling a flower.

CAR

Hands move in action of holding and moving a steering wheel.

MOTORBIKE

Fists twist from palm down to palm forward sharply twice.

Other signs can be considered to be indirectly iconic in that a typical feature of the object being referred to is used to refer to the whole object.

The examples here show the beak of a **bird**, the trunk of an **elephant**, the ears of a **rabbit** and so on to represent the animals referred to in these signs.

Actions associated with particular objects can also be used to depict that object, as in **flower**, **car** and **motorbike**.

ICONICITY (translucent)

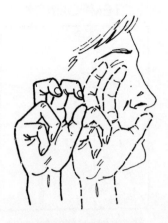

QUICK

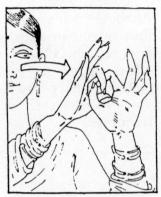

R. index hits L. index and bounces sharply up.

SLOW

R. index moves slowly up left arm.

The examples on the previous two pages have shown iconicity in relation to physical objects in which the visual representation can be readily seen and can be described as transparently iconic.

CONTACT

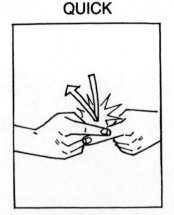

R. hand moves towards L. and fingers of 'O' hands interlock.

PROOF

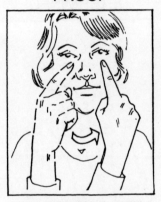

Tip of index makes contact beneath one eye and then the other.

Ideas that are less concrete can also involve a degree of iconicity that, although not immediately obvious to learners, can be accepted as iconic once the meaning has been given.

KEEN

Fingers bent at second knuckles; hands rub up and down alternately on chest in short, quick movements.

BORED

Hand taps just below mouth several times as if stifling a yawn.

The signs illustrated on this page show a degree of iconicity that can be described as translucent, although different degrees of iconicity are very much open to individual interpretation.

ARBITRARY SIGNS

BECAUSE

L. flat hand, thumb up. Bring R. flat hand down onto edge of L. index, then tap against L. thumb.

DETERMINED

R. 'R' hand, palm left held at side of face, twists so tip touches chin.

GOING TO

Thumb extended, held on upper trunk, prods into body in two small quick movements.

Although many signs have their origins in visual imagery or symbolism, many others appear to be completely arbitrary, like most of the words of spoken languages.

Signs change over time and this can have the effect of lessening any iconic links to meaning they may have had.

The examples shown here are of signs that appear to be completely arbitrary. They may have originated in a purely arbitrary way, or have had visual links to meaning that have become submerged over time until they are no longer visible.

TEMPORARY

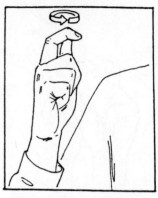

Thumb tucked into bent index. Hand moves in small circles.

NURSERY

Tip of extended middle finger taps chin twice.

REASON

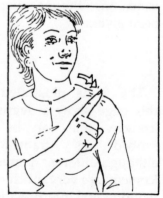

Edge of R. index contacts L. shoulder twice.

ORIGINS OF SIGNS

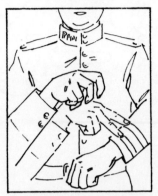

Fingers of R. 'V' hand pull
across L. wrist and flex.

When learning a foreign spoken language, we may rarely question the origins of its words, or ask 'Why is that the word for . . . ?', and yet hearing people learning BSL tend to do this, as if an explanation for a sign's origin should always be possible. There has been a tendency for those teaching 'signing classes' in the past to offer possible explanations, which may or may not be appropriate to the learning of a language.

DETECTIVE

Hand twists from wrist in action
of turning lapel over.

However, hearing learners claim that such explanations act as a mnemonic which helps them to remember signs. The examples here start with **police**, said to originate from the stripes along the cuffs of the early police uniform. **Detective** indicates turning back the lapel to reveal a pin or badge on the other side, as worn at one time by detectives. The origins of the sign **social worker** relate to the church-based missioner, and the outline of the stole, a vestment worn across the shoulders.

SOCIAL WORKER

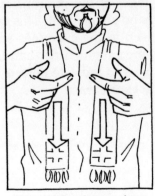

Tips of 'C' hands move down
upper chest.

These examples are interesting because of their historical associations, but it is not necessary to know them. Young Deaf people using the signs are unlikely to have heard of the suggested origins, and have acquired them as arbitrary representations in the same way that hearing children learn words.

CLASSIFYING HAND SHAPES: FLAT SURFACES

The introduction to this section mentions the fact that sign language is able to compact information into individual sign units through such devices as modulation, placement and non-manual information carried by the face, eyes and body.

Groups of hand shapes known as CLASSIFIERS actually incorporate specific detail of the referent by the hand shape itself. This can be seen in the examples shown here in which flat hands are used to indicate objects with flat surfaces.

ROOF

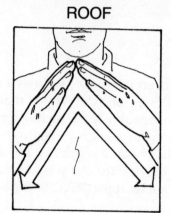

Flat hands move down/out in shape of roof.

MIRROR

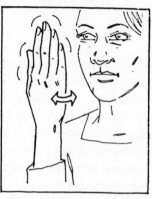

Flat hand makes small quick twisting movements in front of face.

FLOOR

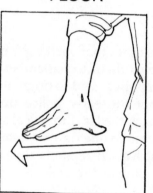

Palm down flat hand moves horizontally.

DOOR

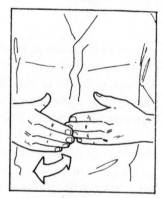

R. flat hand swings to contact L. flat hand.

CORRIDOR

Flat hands held apart palms facing, move forward.

WALL

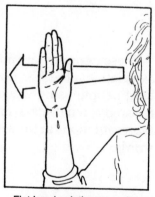

Flat hand pointing up makes sweeping movement to indicate surface of wall.

CLASSIFYING HAND SHAPES: HANDLING/GRASPING

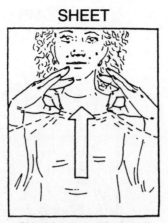

SHEET

'O' hands move up body as if drawing up a sheet.

BLANKET

Fists move up body as if pulling up a blanket.

One group of classifying hand shapes is based on the handling or grasping of various objects, either in whole or in part.

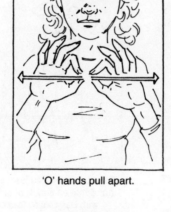

WIRE

'O' hands pull apart.

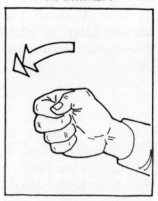

HAMMER

Closed hand moves in action of holding and using a hammer.

Dimensions such as thickness or weight can be indicated by the particular hand shape used. An 'O' hand in which the thumb and index form a circle occurs in signs for fine or lightweight objects, as in **sheet**, **wire** and **needle**.

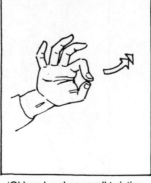

NEEDLE

'O' hand makes small twisting movement.

IRON

Palm down fist moves from side to side.

The handling of heavier or thicker objects is frequently indicated by a closed hand or fist, as in **blanket**, **hammer** and **iron** shown here.

49

CLASSIFYING HAND SHAPES: HANDLING/GRASPING

COMB

Thumb tucked into bent index; hand moves in action of combing.

BRUSH

Fist moves in action of brushing.

BADMINTON

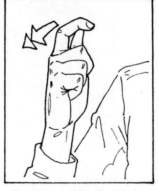

Thumb tucked into bent index; hand makes action of striking with badminton racket.

TENNIS

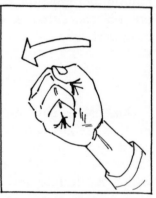

Fist moves in action of striking with tennis racket.

LOLLY

Thumb tucked into bent index, makes short movements near chin.

ICE-CREAM

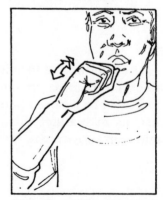

Fist held near chin makes short movements.

Objects of medium weight and thickness frequently incorporate the hand shape used here in **comb**, **badminton** and **lolly**, in which the thumb is tucked into the bent index.

This gives a degree of contrast between these lighter objects and the heavier ones they have been paired with, depicted in these examples by a fist in **brush**, **tennis** and **ice-cream**, in which the main differentiating feature is the hand shape.

Groups of signs for objects like these rely on the correct hand shape being used to portray the comparative width and weight by which such items can be distinguished.

CLASSIFYING HAND SHAPES: DISCRIMINATING SIZE

The examples shown here give a good illustration of the use of the hand shapes described on the previous two pages. All can be used to indicate painting, but the choice of hand shape can provide very specific information concerning the implement used to paint with, relevant to the context.

For example, the top illustration shows an 'O' hand being used, and would be relevant to **painting with a small, fine brush**. The middle illustration uses the hand shape in which the thumb is tucked into the bent index, and would be relevant to **painting with a medium-sized paint brush**. The bottom example uses a fist, and would be relevant to **painting with a paint roller**.

In this way, the information conveyed is not merely the act of painting, but gives quite precise detail of the implement used, in a way that the English word 'paint' alone cannot do, giving a glimpse of how sign language can incorporate information into single sign units, even when uninflected, like those illustrated here.

CLASSIFYING HAND SHAPES: PEOPLE AND VEHICLES

EYE GAZE

There is a further group of classifying hand shapes whose function is similar to the use of pronouns in English, although there is no precise counterpart. There is a number of different hand shapes that function in this way and the illustrations here show some frequently used examples. The same hand shape may be used for more than one class of referent — for example, the closed hand is also used as a classifier indicating possession and the 'V' hand as a classifier representing both the path of eye gaze, and leg movement.

PERSON

PEOPLE

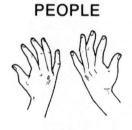

As with other groups of classifiers, the hand shape in these examples provides information on the type or class of referent. This can then be used to refer to objects or people that have not been named, or to refer back to such items after they have been identified. In particular they can be manipulated to indicate locations of people, or objects in space, and show the manner, direction or rate of movement in a way that mirrors the person or object in reality.

LEGS

HEAD/MASS

The hand shapes themselves are part of the conventionalised patterns of BSL, whereas their individual use may incorporate an element of mime.

VEHICLE

CLASSIFYING HAND SHAPES: PERSPECTIVE

Both hands using the PERSON classifier are shown here in the top examples, **meet** and **swap** (as in 'swap places').

The middle pair of examples shows the LEGS classifier in **jump** and **lie down**.

The bottom examples are of the closed hand shape representing head movement. Its use in **refuse** can emphasise and add stress to accompanying head movement, where **loss of face** shows a more figurative use.

Switches between these classifiers allow changes in perspective, from the movement of the whole person, to the more detailed perspective of leg and head movement. Other classifiers can give even closer detail of movement of the eyes, mouth or feet.

MEET

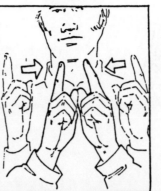

Index fingers move towards each other.

SWAP

Index fingers held apart swap places with each other.

JUMP

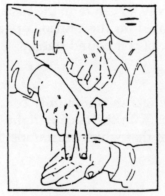

R. 'V' hand makes small jumping movements on L. palm.

LIE (down)

Palm up R. 'V' hand makes small movement along L. palm.

REFUSE

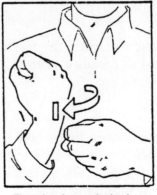

Fist twists from palm back to palm forward emphatically.

LOSS OF FACE

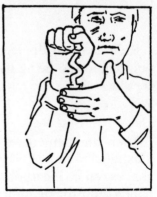

R. fist moves down behind L. flat hand with small side to side wavering movement.

COMPOUND SIGNS

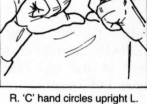

COMMUNITY

R. 'C' hand circles upright L. index.

Classifying hand shapes, as already mentioned, can be used in a freely descriptive way, or can form the basis of signs, such as those illustrated on the previous page. They also occur in a number of compound signs.

The extended left index finger in **community** can be seen as the person classifier, with the circling right 'C' hand giving an indication of that which surrounds the individual.

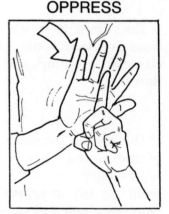

OPPRESS

R. open hand pushes L. index forward and down.

Oppress again involves the person classifier, indicating the individual being pressed down by external pressures.

Ride involves the legs classifier astride the forward-pointing index, being used in this instance as an animal classifier.

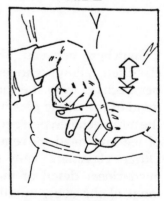

RIDE

R. 'V' hand astride forward pointing L. index.

There are many more examples, and these have been illustrated to show the basic idea of how classifying hand shapes can be incorporated into sign units, so that both hands can provide information simultaneously.

SIMULTANEITY

Moving on from compound signs in which both hands provide information simultaneously, to a phenomenon very particular to sign languages, in which two separate signs, or whole units of meaning, can be articulated at the same time.

The top example on the right shows the signs **deaf** and **born** articulated at the same time, and in the middle illustration, **little** and **girl**.

The bottom example is different. The sign 'fight', normally signed in a fixed location, shows the formation moving up along a 'time line', which is used to refer to 'growing time'. This appeared in a context concerning a brother and sister who were always fighting each other when they were children and could be translated as **they grew up fighting**. This is just one example showing two units of meaning articulated together, in a way that fully exploits the structured use of space to suit individual contexts.

Since this type of structure is not possible in spoken English, it is a crucial area in learning sign language. Learners may be typically looking for 'words' that are not there and missing vital information that is.

DIRECTIONAL VERBS

HELP

R. closed hand with thumb extended, supported and moved forward by L. hand.

HELP

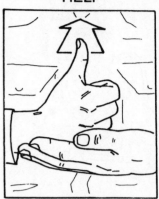

R. closed hand with thumb extended, supported and moved backward by L. hand.

Changes in direction occur in a large number of signs to give context-specific information, particularly in relation to the implied subject and object of certain verbs.

INTERRUPT

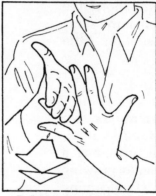

R. flat hand pushes forward between fingers of L. hand.

INTERRUPT

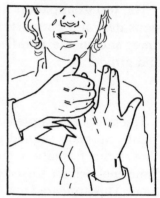

R. flat hand pointing back pushes between fingers of L. hand.

The direction of the movement can simultaneously incorporate such information, as in the examples shown here.

TEACH

Bunched hands twist to point and move forward from near temples.

TEACH

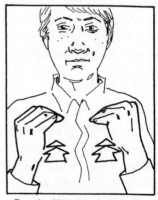

Bunched hands twist to point and move backward to signer in short repeated movement.

The forward movement in **help** shows the signer as the subject, relevant to a context such as 'can I help?' Where the sign moves back towards the signer, the meaning changes and the signer becomes the object, as in 'I was helped'. This same principle applies to **interrupt** and **teach**, in which both direction and orientation change.

BORROWINGS

Palm back flat hand held in front
of face moves forward and twists
to palm forward.

PSYCHOLOGY

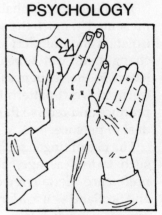

Blade of R. hand taps twice
against base of L. thumb and
index.

No language, whether spoken or signed, is 'pure'.
Languages develop and are influenced by other
languages throughout their history. Part of these influences can be seen in 'borrowings' of words and phrases
from other languages. English is full of such borrowings
— words such as *hamburger* and *kindergarten* from
German, or *chic* and *picnic* from French.

Similarly, other languages borrow from us, as in the
French adoption of 'le weekend'. BSL and other sign
languages do this too.

ANYWAY

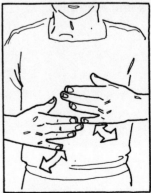

Flat hands swing to and fro
alternately brushing fingertips.

The examples here show **attitude**, borrowed from
Danish Sign Language, and **psychology** and **anyway**,
just two examples of borrowings from American Sign
Language.

FINGER SPELLING

A rich source of borrowing into BSL is the English language which surrounds the Deaf community. Finger spelling is an important part of BSL, but since it provides a letter-for-letter representation of the written alphabet, it relies on familiarity with the English word and should be used with caution.

There are many different written alphabets and different forms of manual alphabets in existence throughout the world. Britain uses a two-handed finger spelling system which originated in the seventeenth century, but the majority of finger spelling systems used by other countries are one-handed forms. (The American one-handed system is illustrated in the Appendices.)

The illustrated alphabet on the following page shows the individually formed letters presented in much the same way as the sign illustrations have been presented, that is, in isolation and uninflected. When seen in fluent use, the individual letters undergo certain changes and can appear quite different, depending, for example, on the surrounding letters in the sequences in which they are used. For this reason, finger spelling is best learnt in word pattern forms, rather than learning the alphabet by rote. The ability to produce and receive fluent finger-spelt patterns as used by Deaf people requires a great deal of practice.

The use of finger spelling within BSL varies considerably between individuals, due to such factors as age, educational background, familiarity with English or personal preference. Certain regions in Britain — for example, some parts of the north of England and Scotland — use a large proportion of finger-spelt words in all contexts, whereas other regions use much less.

Finger spelling can be used to spell out words in full, such as names of places and individuals, or to provide abbreviated forms of words, sometimes simply the initial letter, or a finger-spelt formation can be incorporated into a sign. The following pages provide some examples.

BRITISH TWO-HANDED FINGER SPELLING ALPHABET

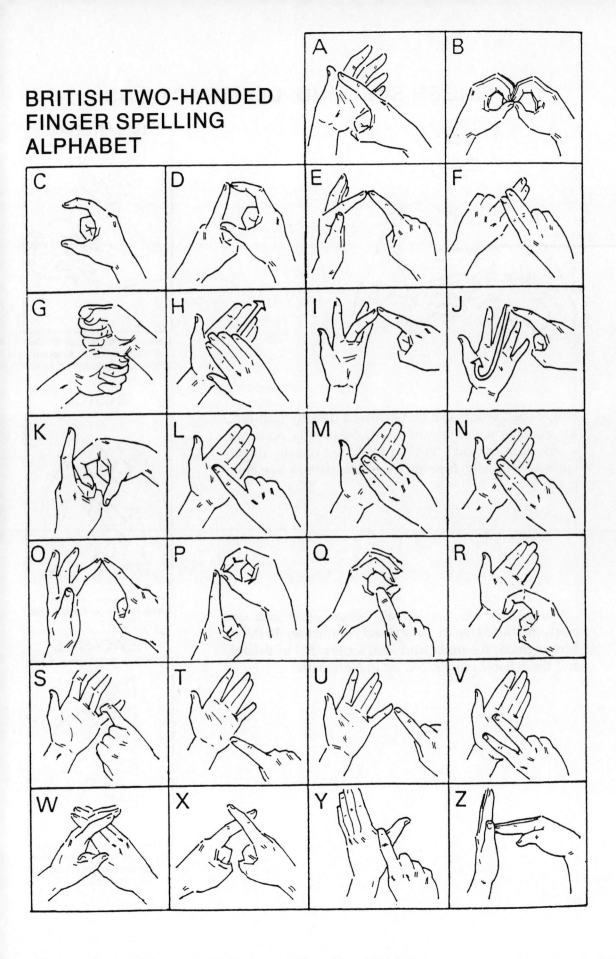

FINGER SPELLING: CONTRACTIONS

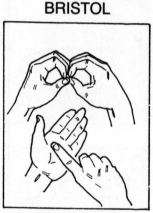

Hands form finger-spelt 'B', then R. hand sweeps in small arc around L. palm to form the letter 'M'.

BRISTOL

Hands form finger-spelt 'B' then 'L'.

NEWCASTLE

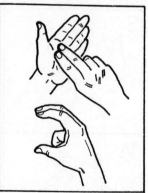

Form finger-spelt 'N', then form 'C' using index, middle finger and thumb.

Finger-spelt words can be borrowed directly into BSL, for example a number of short, frequently occurring words such as 'son', 'but' and 'job' are usually finger-spelt quite rapidly, forming a sign-like pattern (see **club**, p. 68).

Placenames are also usually finger-spelt and are often contracted, as in the stylised contraction 'BHM' in **Birmingham**, the initial and final letters 'BL' in **Bristol**, and the syllable initials 'NC' as in **Newcastle**.

FINGER SPELLING: INITIALISATION

The repeated initial letter is also common in frequently occurring words such as **kitchen** and **daughter**, shown here.

The examples of **gold** and **answer** show a form of initialisation that has become more sign-like by taking on the characteristics of signs in a way that extends the simple initial. This process helps to avoid large numbers of different words being represented by the same initials.

Family and **communicate** are examples in which initialised hand formations have been incorporated into existing signs.

KITCHEN

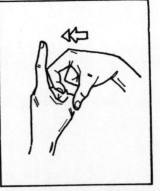

Form finger-spelt 'K' and tap formation together twice.

DAUGHTER

Form finger-spelt 'D' and tap formation together twice.

GOLD

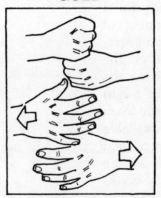

Hands form finger-spelt 'G' then move apart and spring open.

ANSWER

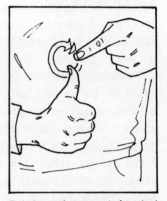

R. index makes repeated contact with tip of L. thumb.

FAMILY

Form finger-spelt 'F' and move formation in horizontal circle.

COMMUNICATE

'C' hands move alternately backward and forward in front of the body.

FINDING OUT MORE

A visual language must be seen to be appreciated, and it is simply not possible to do justice to a language as visually rich as BSL in a static printed medium. However, the intention of this section has been to offer a taster, a brief glimpse of some of the interesting features of BSL at the level of its vocabulary, that might stimulate the reader to want to learn more. **Classes** are now available across the country, taught by trained Deaf tutors who use BSL as the language of instruction, and books can provide a useful reference point for both tutor and student.

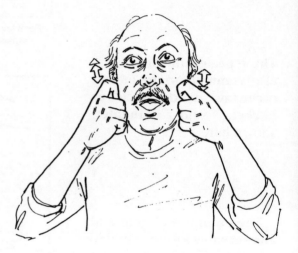

Many of the crucial grammatical features of sign language that help to compact information and carry meaning, such as **non-manual features** (of the face and body), BSL lip patterns, modulation, multichannel signs, placement and other visual **structures**, are not even touched on here. Details can be found in other sources, such as those given at the end of the book.

THE DEAF WORLD:
COMMUNITY AND CULTURE

INTRODUCTION

The previous section considered some aspects of BSL as the primary language of Britain's Deaf Community. As pointed out in the Introduction to this book, the language and culture of all societies are interlinked, each being a reflection of the other, and so it is the Deaf community and the culture shared within it that is introduced in this section.

The desire to learn BSL brings Deaf and hearing people into contact in a way that was not seen even ten years ago. Recognition of the relationship between language and culture has led to the encouragement of students of sign language to gain some experience of Deaf culture, mainly through visits to local Deaf clubs and other forms of social contact.

Like BSL, Deaf culture has been around for a long time, but has only been recognised and talked about in very recent years. Until about seven years ago, there was no sign for either *culture* or *community* in BSL, and these new coinages reflect the increased consciousness and sense of identity within the Deaf community, brought about by developments described in more detail in Section Seven.

Culture is a notoriously ambiguous concept which is difficult to define, having different levels and boundaries relevant to different groups within society. The term can be used on a global scale to differentiate, for example, between Eastern and Western culture, or to identify small sections of British society that can be geographically defined as having differences in cultural values, such as may be found amongst Geordies, Cockneys, Scousers and others. Boundaries are not only geographically defined but also exist on various levels, to identify life-styles that separate class cultures, youth cultures, or that mark various religious cultural groups.

Deaf culture can also be seen on several levels. Many Deaf households contain special aids and equipment that may be completely outside the experience of hearing people (see Section Five) but play an important part in Deaf people's lives. The language of Sign itself brings with it very real differences. There is a lot of physical movement compared to spoken language, with hands and arms seeming to fly everywhere and a profusion of shifting facial expressions rarely seen in hearing society. Deaf people may stand or group themselves differently for easier sign production and reception. Good visibility is important and there are specific rules about turn-taking, interrupting and gaining attention, that hearing learners need to be made aware of to avoid causing offence. It is also considered rude for hearing people to talk among themselves, without signing, when in Deaf people's company.

Deaf people's approach in referring to other people is very visual. Pointing may be used, or physical characteristics indicated, such as size, weight, hair style, facial characteristics, clothes, and so on, rather than a person's name, with some becoming permanent 'name signs' for those individuals within the community. This seems quite natural to a community whose first language is visual and not word-based, since names are themselves words, but hearing people may find it unusual, or even embarrassing, since such actions might be considered rude in hearing circles. Cultural sensibilities can be unexpectedly different.

All the aspects of culture so far mentioned can be seen, but there is another level — that of the shared experience of growing up Deaf, bringing with it shared values, interests and ways of viewing things that are not easy for outsiders to understand or participate in. This may partly explain the concern felt by some Deaf adults that most of the major decisions that affect their lives are made by hearing people who may view things from a quite different perspective.

In the hearing world cultural values, like the accents and dialects of the spoken languages that help to transmit them, are absorbed by children from those around them, providing an identity and sense of belonging that is passed from one generation to the next. What makes the situation so different for deaf children is that they are potentially part of two worlds and two cultures, needing access to both from an early age for a healthy identity as a Deaf person within a hearing society.

The values and beliefs that we grow up with are very much part of our being, often staying with us for life. New cultures can challenge our basic assumptions, an experience that can be both threatening and exhilarating. For many hearing learners, the first visit to a Deaf Club can be something of a culture shock. The feelings of being an outsider, of alienation, cannot be fully explained by the language difference alone, and a common assumption is that this is how Deaf people must feel in the hearing world.

Ninety per cent of Deaf people are born into hearing families and grow up in the predominantly hearing world. Deaf people may or may not feel alienated in some situations, but it would seem unlikely that their experiences would be the same. In addition, they may also be unaware that hearing people might feel like this, since Deaf people make assumptions about hearing people too. However, the idea of sharing language and culture between the Deaf and the hearing world provides a challenge that is there to be explored and enjoyed.

THE BRITISH DEAF COMMUNITY

Deaf people whose primary language is BSL form the nucleus of Britain's Deaf Community. This is not a **community** in the sense of people living in close proximity to each other, but rather in the sense of shared values and experiences and, above all, a shared language.

The Deaf community is held together by such factors as **self-identification** and acceptance by others as a member; by language, marital patterns and a number of national, regional and local organisations and social structures (see Section Six). A person's actual degree of hearing loss is not important in determining identification with or acceptance by the Deaf community; it is more a case of attitude and commitment.

Hearing people may also be accepted as members, particularly children of Deaf parents who have grown up with BSL as a first language, and professionals such as social workers and interpreters who may not be native signers, but have acquired skill in BSL as a second language, and respect the values and **beliefs** of Deaf culture.

DEAF CLUBS AND CENTRES

The figure of 90 per cent, which has been given for the number of deaf children born into hearing families, also applies to the percentage of hearing children born to Deaf parents. Although most Deaf adults will choose a Deaf partner, the majority will have hearing children. Most Deaf people also work and live alongside hearing people, and meaningful communication of any depth may be scant. For this reason, many opt to spend their leisure time with other Deaf people.

Deaf Clubs and Centres provide the focal point for Deaf people's social and leisure activities. At the present time there are over 200 such establishments throughout the United Kingdom. These Centres began early in the nineteenth century as places to meet socially and for prayer meetings, gradually spreading from major cities to smaller towns. Originally called Adult Institutes, or Missions, the sign **Deaf Club** (right), which is a derivation of the sign for 'church', reflects the earlier links to church activities. **Club**, as shown at the top of this page, is an example of a stylised finger-spelt contraction.

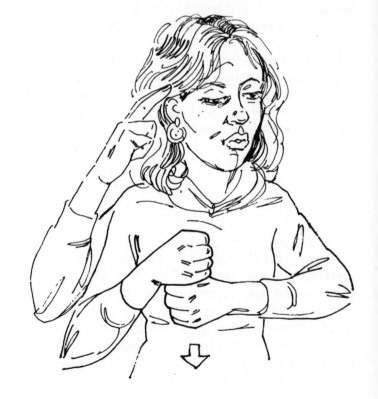

DEAF CLUBS AND CENTRES

Deaf Clubs come in many shapes and sizes, but all provide a place for Deaf people and their families to come together for **relaxed interaction** in their preferred language of BSL, and away from the pressures of coping with spoken language.

Although between a quarter and a third of profoundly deaf people rarely attend Deaf Clubs, they are clearly valued by those who do, even though they may represent only a small fraction of their lives in terms of actual time spent there. Small Clubs in rural areas may only open one night a month, whereas larger city Clubs might be open every evening.

Most Clubs are run by **committees** made up of elected members who are responsible for fund-raising, the general management of the Club, and for organising activities both locally and nationally. Links with other Clubs and National Organisations provide the basis of the **National** Deaf Community.

CLUB ACTIVITIES

Although not the only focus of Deaf interaction, Clubs do provide a regular **social** meeting place for adults and children (deaf and hearing), and opportunities to meet new people, make relationships and marry. Most Clubs have bars and games rooms, similar to any social club, and can cater for diverse interests, depending on the size of the membership, with a traditional emphasis on sporting activities.

Even before the availability of special text telephones for deaf people (like the Minicom described on p. 85), Clubs provided a hive of activity and discussion, with news and information that could spread across the whole country in a matter of days.

Like all social groups, the Community is dynamic and changing. Some of the current trends reflect the increased interest in BSL and through that the Community and its culture. This has led to a marked increase in the number of **hearing people** attending Deaf Clubs, particularly as more and more Deaf people are training as BSL tutors. This has also added to a growing Deaf cultural consciousness, with regional **debating** groups in some parts of the country.

DEAF CULTURE

The sign **culture** shown opposite is a relatively new coinage, giving some indication of the recent heightened cultural consciousness within the Deaf community. Previously, Deaf people used the term the 'Deaf Way', which gives a useful description of culture, since it embraces a whole way of life and way of viewing things.

It is impossible to make hard-and-fast rules where communities are concerned, but early childhood deafness, with its singular effects on language and communication, does appear to be the chief identifying characteristic of core membership. Deaf people sometimes express in BSL the idea of **'growing up Deaf'**, giving some indication that deafness is part of their total childhood experience, their entire being.

The whole shared **experience** of growing up Deaf is what makes the Community so unique, giving a different perspective on life, even to the extent that deafness itself is rarely seen as a problem. This can bring about the shared feeling of belonging and sense of closeness that leads Deaf people to seek each other out.

DEAF CULTURE: SCHOOLS

Schools for the deaf have an important place in Deaf people's lives, and the most frequently asked question when Deaf people first meet each other is 'Which **school**?' Language and culture are principally **passed down from one generation to the next**, and it is from other deaf youngsters that children first start to acquire this sense of belonging.

In spite of the poor educational achievements described in Section One, deaf schools are the environments in which sign language and identity start to become established (even where official school policy does not include signing). Language and culture flourish here amongst the children, even in the absence of adult role models.

Schools provide the first experiences for most deaf children of a community environment where confidence in communication can be enjoyed. The shared **values** and relationships formed here can last a lifetime.

THE HEARING WORLD

Section Two points out that Deaf people live simultaneously in the Deaf and the hearing worlds, with both sides making adjustments to the communication needs of a particular situation. However, the more complex and serious the exchange, the greater the need for a fully shared language, and for most Deaf people, this will be BSL. Since this is not the language of the majority, an intermediary, such as an interpreter, may be required.

Deaf people have a need for access to spoken or written information in numerous situations, such as further and higher **education**, in the legal and **health** services, **employment** interviews, meetings, conferences, and so on.

In the past, Deaf people generally used friends and relations to interpret for them in dealings with hearing people, and for many this informal network of help is still important in providing interpreting support. Formal support through social workers is also commonly used, although there is now a move to separate interpreting from social work services.

THE PROFESSIONS: INTERMEDIARIES; INTERPRETERS

The rapidly increasing demand for formal interpreting **services** at present far outstrips the supply, but a number of professions are emerging to provide such services across the range of language and **communication** modes between BSL and English. These include registered qualified British Sign Language/English **interpreters** and registered trainee interpreters, lip-speakers and interpreters in deaf–blind communication.

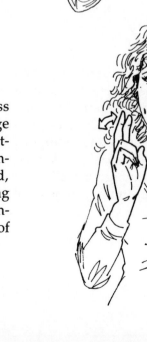

The term 'interpret' refers to the process of relaying a message from a source language (for example, BSL) to a target language (for example, spoken English), either consecutively, or more often simultaneously. The term is also sometimes used in relation to lip-speakers and others who process information in spoken or signed English, operating between different modes rather than different languages.

Interpreters are required to operate across a wide spectrum of situations, from large public gatherings to closely intimate settings. This calls for a high level of competence in the languages concerned, together with training in the interpreting process, and appropriate professional conduct, as reflected in the Interpreter's Code of Practice.

THE PROFESSIONS: TEACHING; SOCIAL WORK

Although a wide variety of **professionals** has contact with Deaf people at various times, few of these will have had any formal training in deafness. Some professionals, such as specialist **teachers** and **social workers**, have a direct role with Deaf people, but only in the case of teachers of the deaf is training in deafness mandatory. None of the professions, with the exception of interpreters, has any compulsory requirements to demonstrate that its members can communicate with Deaf people.

In addition, the training requirements of some professions make it difficult for Deaf people to become practitioners — 96 per cent of teachers of the deaf, for example, are hearing people. Although the exact number of Deaf people involved in interpreting and social work services is not known, the majority are hearing.

Some specialist professionals are native signers, particularly in the field of social work and interpreting. However, there is a general tendency greatly to underestimate the task of acquiring BSL as a second language, putting unrealistic expectations on non-native signers to 'pick it up as they go along', in the absence of adequate training opportunities.

PRACTICAL EQUIPMENT

INTRODUCTION

Part of the Deaf experience involves various practical environmental aids that form part of everyday life in many Deaf households and places of work, and as such will naturally crop up in conversation from time to time. A comment such as, 'I was on the Minicom last night, when the lights flashed', can evoke some colourful imaginings by unsuspecting hearing learners unfamiliar with such situations, and possibly unaware that this simply means that someone came to the door whilst the 'speaker' was on the telephone.

This section looks at some of the most commonly used aids to everyday living which may be found in any deaf home or workplace. These can be put into three categories:

a) LISTENING DEVICES, such as television adaptors and loop systems, which enable partially deaf and hard of hearing people to listen to the television and radio, and to take part in conversations.

b) ALERTING DEVICES, such as doorbell systems, vibrating and flashing alarm clocks, and smoke detector units.

c) TELECOMMUNICATION SYSTEMS, such as textphones and teletext television.

Practical products such as these do much to facilitate independence, particularly important for young Deaf people in hearing families. Local Social Services Departments (Social Work Departments in Scotland) have a responsibility to provide environmental aids for use in the home. They are normally provided on free loan, but availability varies according to the policies and financial budgets of individual areas. The Disablement Advisory Service at the Job Centre can provide a similar service to deaf people in, or seeking, employment.

Such equipment can also be purchased privately. Technical details or suppliers are not given here, but are available from a variety of sources, some of which are given in the Useful Addresses at the back of the book.

LISTENING DEVICES:
TELEVISION, RADIO AND CONVERSATION

Amplification is frequently thought to answer the needs of all deaf people, but making sounds louder does not benefit those with profound deafness and does not overcome the problem of distortion that is present in most types of deafness.

However, many hard of hearing and partially deaf people do make use of a range of amplifying, or **listening**, devices, either independently or in conjunction with hearing aids.

Hearing aids amplify sound, but do not discriminate between wanted sound (the message) and unwanted sound (background noise or competing messages), and have a limited ability to pick up sound from varying distances. Listening devices can be of help to the user (without disturbance to others) by providing increased volume that reduces the problems of distance and unwanted noise.

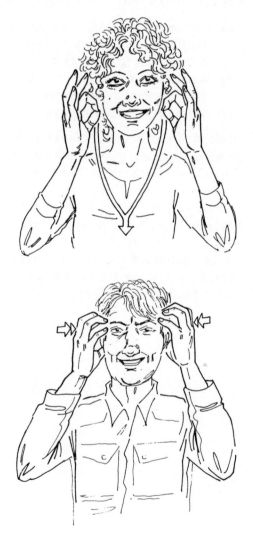

There is a number of different adaptors for use with the television, music centre, radio and for conversational purposes. These include microphone or plug-in **adaptors** and **amplified headphones**, that can be used independently or with loops and infra-red systems (which can also be used in conjunction with hearing aids).

LISTENING DEVICES: AUDIO INDUCTION LOOP SYSTEMS

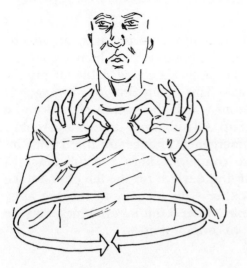

Noisy environments can make it difficult for anybody to hear clearly and without strain, but for a person wearing a hearing aid it may be almost impossible. The limitations of hearing aids in terms of unwanted noise and distance can be greatly alleviated by **loop systems**. A loop system involves a loop of wire around an area such as a room or hall, which connects to an amplifying unit attached to the sound source. This can be connected to a television in the home, for example, or to a sound system in public meeting places such as theatres, lecture halls and churches.

A magnetic field is formed within the looped area, and the amplified sound can be picked up directly by hearing-aid users provided they remain within the area of the loop and have either a hearing aid that has a switch with a 'T' position, or a special listening device as mentioned on the previous page.

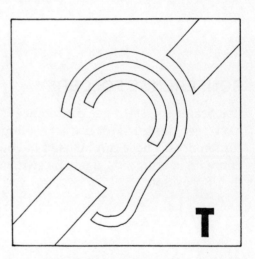

Loop systems are increasingly being used in public places of all kinds, and offer a relatively inexpensive and effective means of providing better quality of sound directly to the user, that can minimise background noise and allow freedom of movement within the area, without creating any discomfort for others. There are also systems which use infra-red technology instead of wiring.

People able to use loop systems should look for the above symbol in public buildings. This **international symbol of deafness** (normally on a maroon background) is the same as that used to advertise the Sympathetic Hearing Scheme administered by the British Association of the Hard of Hearing (see p. 94) with the addition of the letter 'T', and is available from the Royal National Institute for Deaf People.

LISTENING DEVICES: TELEPHONE

The 'T' switch on hearing aids can also be used on telephones with inductive couplers which are now widely available for private purchase. This again provides a magnetic field from which the speech signal can be picked up. All public pay phones and motorway emergency phones are fitted with inductive couplers. There is a full range of **amplifying devices for the telephone** to be used either with or without hearing aids, available either built-in or which can be added to certain phones.

CONFERENCE FOLDERS

Practical and easy-to-use **conference folders** have been designed for use at meetings and conferences. These can be used in conjunction with hearing aids, again by switching to the 'T' position.

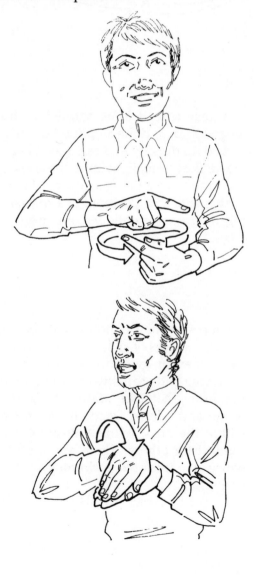

Sound is transmitted from an induction loop amplifier, through a loop cable incorporated in the pad holder within the folder. The pad may be removed from the folder clips and placed wherever desired for maximum comfort and performance. A neck loop is also provided as an alternative output device.

ALERTING DEVICES: DOOR BELLS

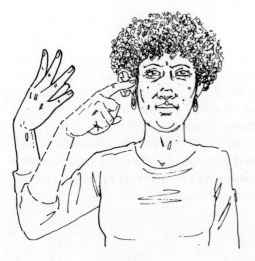

There is a wide range of devices available to deaf people who find conventional bells and alarms ineffective, and these fall into two main categories. Hard of hearing and partially deaf people may prefer to make use of **extra loud** doorbells and alarms of different types, whereas profoundly deaf people may require visual or vibrating indicators.

Amongst these is the visual, or **'flashing light' doorbell**, which alerts a deaf person that someone is at the door. It may be wired to the mains or work on batteries, and can affect all the house lights or be connected to a separate fixed or portable light.

Mains-wired systems affect all the house lights. They can be set to flash on during the day, and to flash off or to dim during the evening, in response to the door bell being pressed or to the **telephone ringing**.

A small number of vibrating indicators is available, which are also suitable for other devices, such as smoke detector alarm units. The vibrating sensation is of particular use to deaf–blind people, and also for use at night.

ALERTING DEVICES: ALARMS

The idea of substituting, or converting, an auditory signal into a visual or vibrating one is also the basis of a wide range of alerting devices, such as **alarms**, most of which can be battery or mains operated.

Special alarm clocks are available which are fitted with either a **flashing light**, or with a **vibrating pad** which can be placed under the pillow or mattress.

The need to be alerted to a crying **baby**, or an invalid in a separate room, can be met by an alarm that flashes or vibrates in response to sound. A microphone placed near the sound source (such as a cot in the case of a baby alarm) will activate the alarm by changing the audible signal into a visual one. The sensitivity of the microphone can be adjusted so that only the sound required will trigger the flash or vibration, and it will also reflect visually the type and duration of the sound, such as short or intermittent, or long and persistent, to give parents some idea of how urgent the cry is.

This type of indicator can also be used to respond to a wide range of sounds such as telephone or doorbell ringing, or an ordinary alarm clock or fire alarm.

TELECOMMUNICATIONS: TEXT TELEPHONES

Among the new technological developments, **text telephones** such as Vistel, Qwerty and Minicom have had a big impact on communications within the Deaf community, making possible telephone contact between profoundly deaf people and other deaf or hearing people with text 'phones, through a rapidly developing regional and national network.

The electronic terminals provide a small keyboard and screen on which incoming and outgoing messages are displayed. The normal telephone receiver is placed on two cups above the keyboard, as indicated in the sign above. The smallest, easiest to use and cheapest terminal is the Minicom, which can run on rechargeable batteries, or on the mains. Being portable, Minicoms can be used on almost any 'phone, including public 'phones. Top of the range versions have ansaphone facilities and a pocket-sized model.

To enable calls to be made to people without a terminal, the RNID runs a national **relay** service called TYPETALK, which operates a 24-hour service, every day of the year. It provides a communication link between deaf, deaf–blind or speech impaired people with text telephones and those who use a standard voice 'phone. This large national service is funded by British Telecom. There is no registration fee and calls are charged as though dialled direct.

Another RNID-run scheme, also funded by British Telecom, is the Text Users Rebate Scheme which is available to help with the increased 'phone bills engendered by the extra time taken by text 'phone calls. The rebate is currently 60 per cent of the call charge portion of the bill, up to £160 per year; it is payable to deaf people who can only use text 'phones, and is confined to domestic use. Contact the RNID for up-to-date details.

Minicom users anywhere in the United Kingdom can summon the emergency services through the National Emergency Call Service (0602 670 100).

TELECOMMUNICATIONS: TEXT TELEVISION

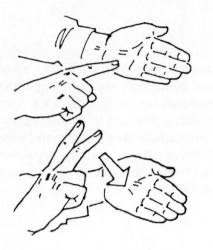

Television is a major source of information in most households. Advances in information technology have greatly increased deaf people's access not only to general information, but to items of specific interest to the Deaf community. Amongst the most significant of these advances are teletext information pages and subtitling facilities.

Teletext is a means of transmitting information which can be picked up and decoded by special TV sets. Certain computer decoders, and a number of video recorders, can also change an ordinary set to one capable of receiving teletext. Information can be in the form of pages of text on the screen in place of the picture, or of subtitles superimposed onto the normal picture. These facilities can be summoned by keying in relevant page numbers on a special remote control unit as indicated in the sign opposite.

Teletext sets now cost little more than ordinary colour TV sets and give deaf people direct **access** to up-to-date news, travel information, sports results and other matters of general interest. In addition, there are special information pages for deaf people.

TELETEXT INFORMATION PAGES

News and information of direct relevance to deaf people, their families and all people interested in deaf matters are available through Ceefax and Oracle. 'Read Hear' is broadcast daily on BBC2, and updated twice weekly. Ceefax page 710 gives an index of topics available on the magazine, which contains approximately 40 pages a week. Channel 4's 'Deafview', on Oracle page 685, broadcasts daily and is updated three times a week.

Both 'Read Hear' and 'Deafview' provide a valuable way of disseminating information directly to deaf people.

In a magazine format, the items covered include news of interest to the Deaf community, forthcoming events such as BSL and Deaf Awareness **Courses**, workshops, conferences and **meetings**, interpreted theatre performances, deaf school reunions, readers' letters, job vacancies and useful Minicom numbers.

The information is straightforward and factual, for the benefit of both Deaf and deaf-ened people.

TELETEXT SUBTITLING FACILITIES

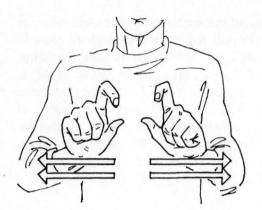

Teletext also provides **subtitles** on certain programmes on all four channels. Some of the most popular and talked-about peak-time programmes are covered and are available by keying 888. A weekly guide to subtitled programmes can be found on Ceefax page 714 which provides details of relevant programmes on all channels. Newspaper television guides and radio and television magazines also indicate subtitled programmes.

Subtitles provide a version of the script including details of sound effects, and may be edited to allow the viewer sufficient reading time. BBC programmes use different-coloured text to identify the main characters, the key to which is given whenever possible at the beginning of the programme.

Subtitles which are available by keying 888 in this way are termed '**closed** subtitles', as they are only available through teletext. '**Open** subtitles' or 'In-vision' subtitles are those that appear on any television set, such as on programmes made for deaf people, or as translations on foreign language films.

SUBTITLES: POPULAR CULTURE

Programmes that are subtitled naturally provide an incentive for deaf people to watch and talk about them, in the way that popular culture is discussed anywhere. Such access also allows young Deaf people to participate in the wider youth culture, an important factor to Deaf teenagers, even though the present provision is somewhat limited.

Across the four channels, approximately 26 programmes at present are subtitled daily, which represents about 80 hours of subtitling a week. These are predominantly pre-recorded network programmes, but do include some live broadcasts. The new Channel 3 and 5 licencees will be required to subtitle at least 50 per cent of all their programmes by 1998, with the possibility that other channels will follow in the same spirit.

The BBC provides subtitles on certain children's programmes, such as 'Blue Peter' and 'Grange Hill', and on soaps such as **'Neighbours'** and **'EastEnders'**, in addition to various films, news and current affairs programmes.

Channel 4 and ITV cover a similar range, including 'Coronation Street', 'Brookside', 'Survival' and **'Home and Away'**.

DEAF ORGANISATIONS

INTRODUCTION

There are approximately 150 different organisations concerned with deafness. Each one represents a quite distinctive area of work and policy, and together they give some idea of the diverse nature of deafness itself.

This section looks at a number of organisations that play a part in the lives of Deaf, deafened, deaf-blind and hard of hearing people. The first organisations formed the 'Panel of Four', set up in 1972 to review the field of services for deaf people and provide a forum for discussion on services and matters concerning deafness and deaf people. This Panel was disbanded in 1993 and replaced by the United Kingdom Council on Deafness (UKCOD). Twenty-nine organisations were accepted as founder members, giving a larger and more effective umbrella organisation to improve and extend co-operation between member organisations in representing and promoting the interests of Deaf, deafened, hard of hearing and deaf-blind children and adults and their families. UKCOD will act as a forum for discussion and the exchange of information; formulate and promote specific and/or major policies in the field of deafness; promote, foster and develop initiatives for improved services; provide an opportunity to share resources and to work together constructively in areas of common interest.

A few organisations have their own 'name signs' by which they are referred to within the Deaf community. Others are usually referred to by finger-spelling the initial letters in their titles, a factor which can be confusing to learners who may be anticipating words when they see finger spelling. Awareness of the role of such organisations, and familiarity with their name signs and initialised finger-spelt patterns, are an important part of the process of sharing knowledge and experience. Such details are given here, illustrated by relevant sign vocabulary.

THE BRITISH ASSOCIATION OF THE HARD OF HEARING

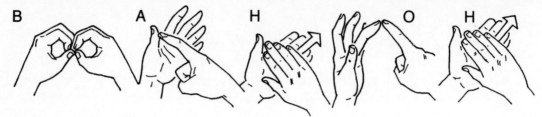

B   A   H   O   H

The British Association of the Hard of Hearing* is a national body for those who have lost all or part of their hearing, and who usually communicate by means of speech supported by lip-reading.

Within the Deaf community, **BAHOH** is normally referred to by its finger-spelt initials. The sign opposite is frequently used to indicate **deafness** in general terms, and also to distinguish deafness occurring after spoken language development, as pointed out in Section One.

BAHOH was founded in 1947 by hard of hearing people themselves, who continue to guide its policies. **Volunteers** are still relied upon for much of its work, which helps to keep costs to a minimum and ensures that it remains, as it always has been, a self-help organisation.

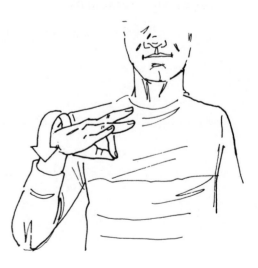

Many Hard of Hearing Clubs throughout the country are affiliated to BAHOH, and can give help and information on support services, and local lip-reading classes.

* In January 1993 this organisation adopted the working title 'Hearing Concern' (British Association of the Hard of Hearing).

94

THE SYMPATHETIC HEARING SCHEME

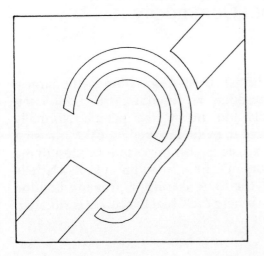

The Sympathetic Hearing Scheme, which is administered by BAHOH, provides training and information on the communication needs of deafened and hard of hearing people. The Scheme does not, at present, include training in sign language, but covers more general awareness and clear communication for those who use speech and lip-reading.

The **international symbol of deafness** shown above (normally on a maroon background) is displayed by a wide variety of organisations, including shops, **banks** and building societies, to indicate that there is a trained member of staff on the premises.

BAHOH and its members wish to promote the use of **lip-speakers**, professionals who act as intermediaries between hearing speakers and lip-readers (see p. 116). Lip-speakers provide a form of interpreting which involves unvoiced repetition of the spoken word in a clear, natural and accurate manner, faithfully reflecting the intention of the speaker. Lip-speaking is a skilled service with three recognised levels of competence leading to membership of the Register of Lip-speakers.

THE BRITISH DEAF ASSOCIATION:
The Voice of The Deaf Community

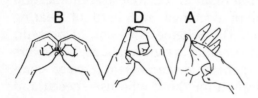

B   D   A

The British Deaf Association is the largest organisation representing the Deaf community and run by Deaf people. Normally referred to by finger-spelling **BDA**, the sign for Carlisle is also important in identifying this organisation. In addition to its **Carlisle** base, the BDA also has a growing **London** office where the Chief Executive is situated.

The BDA's formation came about more than a hundred years ago, as a result of adult Deaf people's concern over developments in deaf education. A resolution to exclude the use of sign languages in deaf schools throughout the world was passed by hearing teachers at the international Milan congress of 1880. In Britain, a Royal Commission into the education of deaf children in 1889 also failed to consult Deaf people, and the exclusion of sign language and Deaf teachers in deaf schools has continued for almost a century. The resultant fall in standards caused Deaf people to unite in defence of their own interests.

The BDA remains a **grass roots** organisation committed to representing the views and rights of Deaf people, with the official recognition of BSL as one of its major objectives.

DEAF CHILDREN AND YOUNG PEOPLE

The BDA's early concern over deaf education continues to be reflected in its present education policy and programmes for deaf children and young people. Its specific objectives include promoting deaf children's **access to sign language**, adult Deaf role models and the Deaf community and its culture, as well as campaigning to end the restrictions which prevent many Deaf people from training as teachers in deaf education. Some of the BDA's direct services include courses to help deaf pupils to prepare for leaving school, adventure courses for younger children and BSL courses for parents.

The BDA is also committed to developing Youth Services, and to this end has appointed two profoundly Deaf people as Assistant Director for Youth, and Youth Officer. A number of projects have been set up, including a major initiative for Deaf youth **leaders** and their trainers, based in Bradford and Ilkley Community College.

'British Deaf **Awareness**' week is organised by the BDA each year, in addition to ongoing information services, such as the London Deaf Access Project which provides information videos for Deaf people whose first language is BSL, and INTO SIGN which provides details of local signing classes. A Health Education Service aimed at increasing Deaf people's own health awareness and making their needs known within the health service is to be led by the BDA's newest department, AIDS AHEAD.

SIGN LANGUAGE SERVICES

The BDA has striven to make BSL more visible at public events, such as party political conferences, and, along with other organisations, has made representations in **Europe** which have resulted in the European Parliament voting unanimously in 1988 for the official recognition of all indigenous sign languages in the European Community. In addition, the BDA has worked energetically to contribute its knowledge and expertise to the Scientific Commissions of Sign Language and Interpreting to the World Federation of the Deaf.

A number of BDA initiatives have led to important developments such as the setting up of the CACDP and BSLTA (described more fully in Section Seven) which have been instrumental in bringing basic sign language skills to the general public. In recognition of the need for advanced courses not only for BSL tutors and interpreters, but also for specialist teachers, social workers and others, the BDA entered into partnership with the Deaf Studies Research Unit at Durham University to develop an Advanced Diploma/MA qualification in Sign Language Studies.

The BDA also has an **advocacy** role in four main areas. These include supporting individual cases of discrimination, influencing Government policy and legislation, encouraging Deaf people's own advocacy skills, and informing and encouraging positive attitudes to deafness amongst the hearing public.

THE NATIONAL DEAF CHILDREN'S SOCIETY

N    D   C   S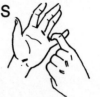

The National Deaf Children's Society is the only national charity specifically concerned with the needs of **deaf children** and their families. Usually referred to by its finger-spelt initials, **NDCS** is based in London and represents deaf children's interests nationally and locally by supporting parents through a large network of self-help groups throughout the country.

The Society provides advice on welfare, education, health and audiology. In addition, it publishes information on all aspects of childhood deafness, and gives grants for holidays, education, research and equipment for children and families in need.

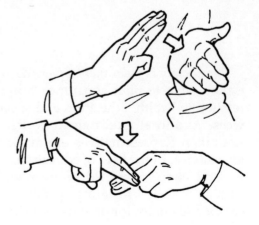

Nationally and locally, professionals including teachers, doctors, audiologists and social workers enter into partnership with **parents**, grandparents, and deaf/Deaf people themselves, to promote the interests of deaf children.

THE NATIONAL DEAF CHILDREN'S SOCIETY

The Technology Information Centre at Birmingham provides a comprehensive **display** of environmental aids. Advice and information is available on equipment and technology for deaf children at home and at school, with the opportunity to see and try out various pieces of equipment. The Blue Peter lend-an-aid library and the children's equipment fund are organised by 'TIC'.

To improve access and provide a more national service, a third Centre has been opened at Leeds. The Family Services Centre concentrates on a range of family support, including help for **families** with special needs. Personal help is available with reviews and appeals, in addition to a full information service with a lending library and research collection.

The Society is essentially a parents' organisation, able to offer consumer support in relation to health, education and social services. At a local level trained Welfare and Education Representatives are available to give **advice**. In the field of education, NDCS is particularly committed, as were its founders in 1944, to fostering quality in education and choice for parents and children.

THE ROYAL NATIONAL INSTITUTE FOR DEAF PEOPLE

R   N   I   D

The Royal National Institute for Deaf People (RNID) is the largest organisation concerned with deafness, embracing anyone with a hearing loss, irrespective of degree, ranging from those who were born deaf to those who have become deafened or hard of hearing in later life.

Normally referred to by its finger-spelt initials, the **RNID** is based in **London**, and in recent years has opened regional offices in various parts of the United Kingdom. It provides a range of services in six main areas: residential care, training, information, communication support, specialist telephone services and practical products for deaf and hard of hearing people.

It is generally acknowledged that the RNID has the most comprehensive **library** on deafness in the world, containing books concerned with all aspects of hearing, sound, speech and language. Further information about the library is available from the RNID.

THE ROYAL NATIONAL INSTITUTE FOR DEAF PEOPLE

The RNID produces a comprehensive **Information** Directory providing contact addresses of services available for deaf people, such as schools and units, social workers, Deaf clubs, residential centres and **hostels**. The Directory is updated annually. In addition to this, information about services is provided by staff both in London and in the regions.

The RNID also produces a number of publications covering various aspects of deafness and communication. A publications list is available free of charge from the Information Services Division.

The RNID is responsible for a number of residential centres for deaf people with a variety of special needs, such as deaf–blind people and young people with behavioural problems.

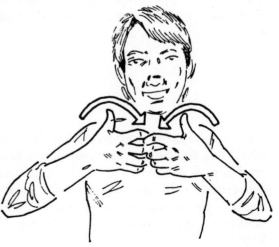

At the present time the RNID is developing interpreter units to give Deaf, deaf/blind and hard of hearing people greater access to information. Practical aids to daily living are developed by the Science and **Technology** Unit.

DEAF ACCORD:
A Consortium of Deaf Consumer Organisations

Deaf **Accord** is an umbrella group of organis-ations of deaf, deaf–blind and hard of hear-ing people. At present these include the BDA, the NDCS and SENSE—the National Deaf–Blind and Rubella Associ-ation.

These organisations are working together to **campaign** for better services, to educate decision-makers and to develop oppor-tunities for younger members. Part of this process involves the work of the Director, in invoking the support of MPs and peers from all parties to influence legislation and im-prove the lives of deaf and deaf–blind people.

Deaf Accord aims to involve **young** people in active roles both within its organisations and in society as a whole. The Young Deaf Achievers Award was set up to acknowledge the outstanding achievements of deaf young people, aged between 16 and 29, which might encourage others and increase public aware-ness of the abilities of young deaf people.

LASER: THE LANGUAGE OF SIGN AS AN EDUCATIONAL RESOURCE

'**LASER**', whose name is an acronym for the Language of Sign as an Educational Resource, was established in 1983 in order to develop the use of sign language in education. The group holds about three workshops a year in different parts of the country, and produces a newsletter called *Laserbeam*.

The emphasis in the **workshops** is on the sharing of information, ideas and experiences, reflecting the range of expertise and skills in the membership. Members include teachers of the deaf, speech therapists, adult Deaf people, parents of deaf children, and others.

LASER WORKSHOP PRINCIPLES

1 BSL has an important role to play in the education of profoundly deaf children, for establishing effective communication.
2 Linguistic competence in BSL can be an important foundation for learning, including the learning of English.
3 Language and English are not seen as synonymous; sign language competence and literacy should be seen as separate skills.
4 English need not be the language used across the curriculum, if information can be more effectively transmitted through sign language.

Bilingual

5 Communication and teaching methods should be seen as separate issues.
6 Deaf adults have an essential contribution to make to the education of profoundly deaf children.

SENSE:
The National Deaf–Blind and Rubella Association

SENSE is a national voluntary organisation which provides services, advice, support and information for deaf–blind children and young adults, their families and professionals in the field. The charity was founded in the 1950s as a self-help organisation for parents of rubella handicapped children. Today, SENSE seeks to enhance the quality of life for all deaf–blind young people, whatever the cause of their dual sensory impairment.

The SENSE Family Advisory Service offers counselling and support from a team of advisory teachers during the crucial early years of a child's development. This may involve home visits, or parents can call into Family Centre bases in London, Birmingham or Glasgow. SENSE also provides rehabilitation, residential further education for young adults and long-term residential care in group homes for **deaf–blind** adults.

The brain receives 95 per cent of all that we know through the senses of sight and hearing — and that means nearly everything. It is very rare to be completely deaf and blind, but the combination of even partial loss of these two crucial senses brings unique problems, requiring specialised services. Causes can be congenital or acquired and include premature birth, birth trauma and **Usher syndrome** — a combination of congenital deafness and gradual loss of sight in early adulthood.

SIGNS OF CHANGE

INTRODUCTION

The changing attitudes to deafness and sign language referred to at the beginning of the book were brought about by a combination of significant factors over the past 15 years or so.

The innovative research work of William Stokoe into American Sign Language (ASL) during the 1960s was to prove influential throughout the world. In this country, two major research projects into British Sign Language were set up in the late 1970s, at Moray House College, Edinburgh and the University of Bristol, both of which involved Deaf native signers on their research teams.

Until this time, Deaf people's communication, generally referred to as 'signing', was held in very low esteem by many hearing people (and indeed by some Deaf people themselves, since it had yet to be recognised as a language). Sign language was widely perceived to be a primitive and restricted code that provided inferior communication in the absence of 'proper language'. This reflected the common hearing image of Deaf people at that time as strange beings who had gross language 'problems' which made them dependent on help from others to get by in life — attitudes that convinced even Deaf people themselves of their inferior status. Not surprisingly, grass roots Deaf people were not seen as being capable of holding positions of responsibility, even in matters directly relevant to their lives and community.

Inspired by what Stokoe had done for the recognition and status of ASL, the British teams sought to identify the sign language used in Britain in a similar way. Even the newly coined term 'BSL' had not been heard of before and was met with suspicion and resistance, many believing that this was a new language that the researchers had invented. In effect, the primary task of the research teams was to put forward evidence that BSL was, in fact, a language and this dominated much of the early research work, with the result that BSL's history as an acknowledged language is very short indeed. However, research began to bring forth evidence that not only is BSL a fully structured visual language, but one of greater depth and complexity than had previously been suspected.

In spite of continued scepticism in some quarters, the gradual dissemination of these findings began the process of change; and as perceptions of sign language started to change, so did perceptions of Deaf people. A start had been made, but radical changes in attitude do not happen overnight and were not brought about by research alone. A number of other progressive developments in the late 1970s and early '80s combined to further influence opinion and fuel the advance.

One of the earliest developments at this time was the use of sign language interpreters at Party Political Conferences, bringing sign language and deafness into the view of the hearing public. Even more significantly, due to deaf people's campaigning work through the Deaf Broadcasting Campaign (formed by the National Union of the Deaf and the

British Deaf Association), sign language became increasingly visible on television. The BBC's 'See Hear!' magazine programme for deaf people first appeared in 1981, followed in 1984 by 'Listening Eye' on Channel 4, a programme with a current affairs approach. In addition to these specialist programmes, BSL interpreters started to appear on other programmes, including some regional news programmes and the Queen's Christmas speech. (Later, in 1988, came the innovative step to teach BSL in the form of the BBC television series 'British Sign Language'.)

The powerful medium of television brought sign language and deafness into the view of the general viewing public, stimulating an unprecedented interest in learning BSL at a time when opportunities to learn were virtually non-existent. Although a number of piece-meal 'signing classes' were in existence in various Deaf Clubs and Centres, these were in the main taught by untrained hearing and deaf people who used speech and taught a signed form of English, reflecting earlier beliefs that BSL was not a real language.

Until the early 1970s, training and examination in sign language interpreting skills were the sole province of the Missioner/Welfare Officers for the Deaf. In view of the intimate nature of the role of these professionals in Deaf people's lives, such skills were considered a fundamental and essential part of their wide-ranging functions and training. Due mainly to new developments in social work training and the setting up of the all-encompassing Social Services Departments, by the mid 1970s even this limited area of provision had disappeared, leaving a void.

At the same time, in the field of deaf education, the evidence of the standards achieved under the predominantly oral system could no longer be ignored. Deaf individuals and organisations were becoming increasingly concerned at the lack of training opportunities and the limited communication skills of those professionals who were at the forefront of providing services to Deaf people and children.

This concern was converted into action by a BDA-initiated Communication Skills Project which sought to promote communication skills amongst the general public and to set up a register of qualified sign language interpreters. This led, in 1982, to the formation of the Council for the Advancement of Communication with Deaf People (CACDP), and gave birth to a national system of examinations in the range of communication methods used by Deaf, deafened and deaf/blind people. Much of the pioneering work was assisted by the Scottish Association for Interpreting for the Deaf, now the Scottish Association of Sign Language Interpreters.

Following a BDA survey into sign language classes in 1982, it was concluded that there was an urgent need to give Deaf people the opportunity of becoming tutors. In 1985, the British Sign Language Tutor Training Agency (BSLTA) was set up in Durham University, with the aim of establishing a training course which would enable Deaf BSL users to become tutors of their own language. For the first time, Deaf people were able to receive training entirely in their first language of BSL, and to realise their true abilities and potential, bringing dramatic changes in attitudes to deafness and BSL and a great boost in confidence for the Deaf Community in general.

RESEARCH

The **research** into BSL and the Deaf community which began in the late 1970s at Moray House College in Edinburgh and the **University** of Bristol has proved an important landmark for Deaf people. The term BSL was not heard of up to this time and its present-day wide acceptance reflects the increasing recognition of sign language as a fully structured language which in turn reflects the respect for and **status** of Deaf people themselves.

Both research teams involved Deaf native signers, but a major turning point in research methods was the advent of inexpensive video equipment which became available at that time. This allowed Deaf people to be filmed signing amongst themselves in natural informal and social settings. In this way, BSL could be observed and later analysed from real-life situations, without the changes and distortions frequently inherent in Deaf people's communication with hearing people. (Earlier attitudes to sign language had convinced even Deaf people themselves that BSL was inferior, causing them to change to more English forms when in contact with hearing people.)

RESEARCH

The availability of a low-priced and easy-to-use means of **recording** allowed the analysis of BSL features that hitherto might have been overlooked or dismissed. New ground had to be broken in finding ways to describe, analyse and transcribe a visual language. Along with new terms like 'BSL' came new sign coinages such as 'classifier', 'iconicity', 'arbitrary' and so on, as illustrated in Section Three.

The process of establishing BSL as a language, with details of its **structures** and functions, had begun, challenging for the first time many of the myths and misconceptions which abounded at this time, not least amongst many professionals in the field.

Research findings and information have gradually been disseminated through courses, lectures, papers, books and videos to have a tremendous **influence** on attitudes to deafness and BSL. For Deaf people this has led to a new sense of confidence, bringing a strengthened identity and pride in the Deaf community.

TELEVISION

Few things have brought deafness into the public eye, and given sign language a **positive image**, as much as television. Deaf people's forte is BSL, which has no written form, but is transmitted live, or through television and video. The visual media are clearly ideal for the transmission of a visual language.

Television is one of the most powerful and influential media in our society, which not only reflects, but helps to create our culture. The increased visibility of BSL on television has brought the image of deafness to hearing as well as deaf **audiences** and in so doing has done more than any other medium in stimulating interest in BSL.

However, this is a recent phenomenon. Prior to the early 1980s there were no regular programmes for Deaf people using sign language, and although teletext was invented in 1974, the first subtitles did not appear until 1981. Recognising the potential of television for the Deaf community, Deaf people began pressing for television access.

TELEVISION: THE DEAF BROADCASTING COUNCIL

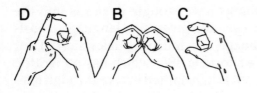

D   B   C

Due to campaigning work by the National Union of the Deaf, a pilot programme for deaf people, entitled 'Signs of Life', was made in 1979 for the BBC's 'Open Door' series. Campaigning continued, with assistance from the BDA, resulting in the formation of the Deaf **Broadcasting** Campaign. 1(The name was changed in 1988 to Deaf Broadcasting Council.)

Usually referred to by its finger-spelt initials, the original aim of the **DBC** was to press for a weekly magazine programme using sign language, subtitles and voice. The role and objectives of the DBC quickly expanded into other areas of television, with the result that it has become a highly respected umbrella consumer organisation representing most of the national organisations for Deaf, hard of hearing and deafened people.

Work continues in persuading broadcasters that all suitable programmes should be subtitled, with some 'open' rather than teletext. More programmes in BSL are also being **pressed for**, using deaf people as presenters and in interpreting roles, in addition to exploring more positive ways in which Deaf and hard of hearing characters can be portrayed.

TELEVISION: DEAF PROGRAMMES

The early campaigning work by the Deaf Broadcasting Council resulted in the first **programmes** made for and with Deaf people, using sign language, subtitles and voice. **'See Hear!'**, a magazine-style programme, was first produced in 1981. A small number of other specialist programmes followed, including, three years later, Channel 4's **'Listening Eye'** series of current affairs-style programmes.

For the first time, Deaf people using sign language were seen presenting and taking part in programmes aimed primarily at Deaf audiences. Many topics of interest and value to Deaf people's lives have been covered since the programmes started, involving studio interviews and location filming of Deaf people throughout Britain.

The programmes have not only received interest from the Deaf community and from deaf and hard of hearing viewers, but have made a significant impact on hearing audiences. Seeing BSL being used on television has stimulated a great deal of interest within the hearing public, resulting in an increased demand for sign language classes throughout the country.

THE COUNCIL FOR THE ADVANCEMENT OF COMMUNICATION WITH DEAF PEOPLE

The Council for the Advancement of Communication with Deaf People, usually referred to by its finger-spelt initials (or sometimes referred to by the name sign **'CAP'**, opposite) is based at **Durham** University and was formally constituted in 1982. Prior to this date, a national system of examinations in sign language did not exist. Earlier training opportunities had been combined with those of the Missioner/Welfare Officer and later Social Worker with Deaf People and were only available to such professionals.

Even this limited provision disappeared during the mid 1970s, causing great concern to Deaf organisations and service users who relied heavily on interpreting services from this source. In response, the BDA initiated a Communication Skills Project, to examine ways of encouraging basic sign language skills among the general public and to establish a register of sign language interpreters, and this in turn led to the formation of CACDP.

The early work of setting up the **register** of sign language interpreters has spread to include lip-speakers and interpreters for deaf–blind people, but CACDP's major significance has been in offering examination opportunities to anybody wishing to learn, providing a tremendous spur and incentive to the acquisition of the whole range of communication skills.

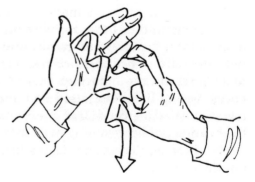

THE COUNCIL FOR THE ADVANCEMENT OF COMMUNICATION WITH DEAF PEOPLE

The CACDP is primarily an examining body, responsible for establishing **examination** procedures in BSL stages 1–3, sign language interpreting, lip-speaking and deaf–blind communication. CACDP's training role applies mainly to training examiners, most of whom are deaf, and offers courses for tutors in the teaching of the **curricula** developed by CACDP for BSL stages 1–3 (Elementary, Intermediate and Advanced) for which accompanying video materials are also available. However, CACDP does not provide general tutor training.

In April 1992 CACDP published a Directory of Sign Language Interpreters which will be updated every year and lists the names, addresses, and qualifications of registered qualified interpreters and registered trainee interpreters. The Directory also explains:

a) The training and qualifications which interpreters need.
b) The recommended fees and working conditions for interpreters.
c) The Code of Practice.
d) The Complaints Procedure.

Such developments have made an important contribution to the recognition and status of BSL and other **communication** modes used by deaf, hard of hearing and deaf–blind people, through which the emerging professions of interpreter and lip-speaker can offer deaf/Deaf people wider access and choice.

TRAINING FOR TUTORS OF BRITISH SIGN LANGUAGE

In spite of the developments brought about by research and the increased visibility of sign language so far described, the resultant surge of interest in learning BSL remained largely unmet. Until the early 1980s, the few signing classes that did exist were virtually all taught by hearing people, or deaf people who used speech. At a time when teaching materials and tutor **training** did not exist, classes mainly taught signed versions of English rather than BSL.

Following the Communications Skills Project, the BDA also carried out a survey into **signing** classes. It was concluded that there was an urgent need to establish introductory BSL classes across the country and to provide Deaf people with the opportunity of becoming **tutors** of their own language.

The establishment in 1985 of the British Sign Language Training Agency at Durham University was seen as a way of addressing both these needs. Although often still referred to by its finger-spelt initials of BSLTA, the course title has been changed to the University of Durham's British Sign Language Tutor Training Course (foundation level).

118

TRAINING FOR TUTORS OF BRITISH SIGN LANGUAGE

For the first time, BSL tutor training offered Deaf people the **opportunity** to study and be examined in their first or preferred language of BSL, an experience that had never been available previously. Course materials and teaching for the foundation level course are presented in BSL, live and on video, by the Deaf staff members of the project team, and the courses involve residential course blocks and distance learning.

The courses draw heavily on current research findings into the structure and functions of BSL, to provide tutors with a thorough knowledge of the language they already use fluently. Through this, training is provided in methods of teaching hearing learners, such as the Direct Experience Method, in which the target language of BSL is used throughout as the language of instruction.

The success of this form of training can be seen in the **positive** attitudes in both Deaf tutors and their students, with greatly **improved** standards and understanding of British Sign Language as a result. The true potential of Deaf people is finally being recognised.

APPENDICES

DEAF—BLIND ALPHABET

The R. hand is represented as that of
the sender forming the letters
onto the passive L. hand
of the deaf—blind recipient.

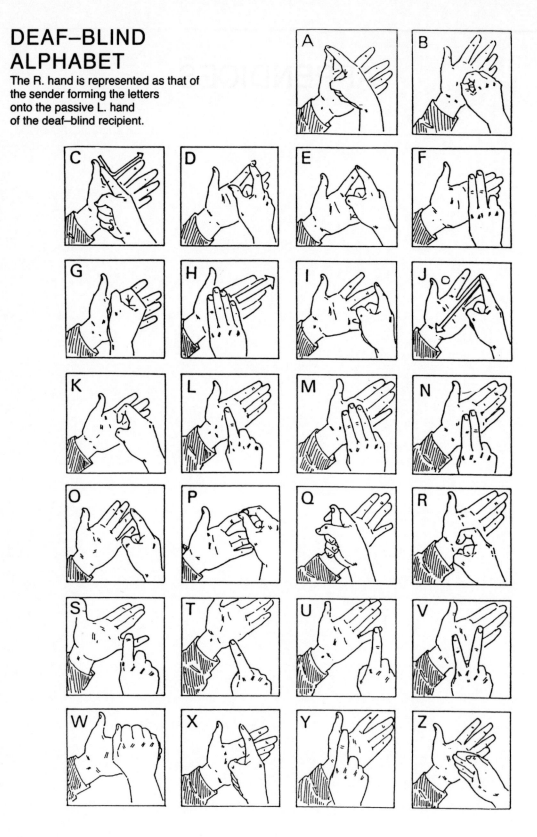

AMERICAN ONE-HANDED FINGER SPELLING ALPHABET

USEFUL ADDRESSES

Alliance of Deaf Service Users and Providers
Centre for Deaf People, Centenary House, North Street, Leeds LS2 8AY. (Tel: 0113 2438328 Voice/Minicom)

Association for the Catholic Deaf of Great Britain and Ireland
Henesy House, 104 Denmark Road, Manchester M15 6JS. (Tel: 0161–226 7139 Voice)

Association of British Sign Language Tutors (ABSLT)
c/o 119, Kingsmead Avenue, Worcester Park, Surrey KT4 8UT.

Association of Sign Language Interpreters (ASLI)
c/o 97, Wesley Close, Harrow, Middlesex HA2 0QE. (Tel: 0181–423 4924 Voice/Minicom)

Association of Teachers of Lip-reading to Adults (ATLA)
Ms Angela Field, Hillsview, Pennsylvania Road, Exeter EX4 5BH. (Tel: 01392 431975)

Breakthrough Trust Deaf Hearing Integration
Selly Oak Colleges, Birmingham B29 6LE. (Tel: 0121–472 6447/471/1001/Voice/Minicom/Vistel)

British Association of Teachers of the Deaf
Icknield High School Hearing Impaired Unit, Riddy Lane, Luton, Bedfordshire LU3 2AH. (Tel: 01582 596599 Voice)

British Deaf Association
1–3 Worship Street, London EC2A 2AB. (Tel: 0171–588 3520 Voice; 0171–588 3529 Text; Fax: 0171–588 3527)

British Society of Hearing Therapists
The Leicester Royal Infirmary, Leicester, Leicestershire LE1 5WW. (Tel: 0116 2541414 ext 5578 Voice)

Centre for Deaf Studies, School of Education
University of Bristol, 22 Berkeley Square, Bristol, Avon BS8 1HP. (Tel: 0117 928 7080 Voice/0117 9251370 Text, Fax: 0117 925 7875)

Church of England Advisory Board of Ministry: Ministry Among Deaf People
Church House, Great Smith Street, London SW1P 3NZ. (Tel: 0171–222 9011 ext 329/223 1153 Voice/Qwerty)

Council for the Advancement of Communication with Deaf People
Pelaw House, School of Education, University of Durham, Durham DH1 1TA. (Tel: 0191–374 3607 Voice and Text, 0191 374 7864 Text Ansaphone, Fax: 0191 374 3605)

Deaf-Blind UK
100 Bridge Street, Peterborough, Cambridgeshire PE1 1DY. (Tel: 01733 358100 Minicom; 01733 358858 Qwerty; Fax: 01733 358356)

Deaf Broadcasting Council
c/o Ruth Myers, 70 Blacketts Wood Drive, Chorleywood, Rickmansworth, Hertfordshire WD3 5QQ.

Deaf Studies Research Unit
University of Durham, Department of Sociology and Social Policy, Elvet Riverside 2, New Elvet, Durham, DH1 3JT. (Tel: 0191–374 2304 Voice, 2314/2306 Text, Fax: 0191 374 4743)

'Deafview'
Tim Russell, 19–23 Featherstone Street, London EC1Y 8SL (Tel: 0171–296 8000 Voice)

The Forest Bookshop: Books on Deafness, Exhibition and Mail Order Specialists
8 St John Street, Coleford, Gloucestershire GL16 8AR. (Tel: 01594 833858 Voice, Text; Fax: 01594 833446)

Friends for the Young Deaf
FYD Communication Centre, East Court Mansion Council Offices, College Lane, East Grinstead, West Sussex RH19 3LT. (Tel: 01342 323444/312639 Voice/Minicom)

Hearing Concern: The British Association of the Hard of Hearing
7-11 Armstrong Road, London W3 7JL. (Tel: 0181–743 1110 Voice/Minicom)

Hearing Dogs for the Deaf
Training Centre, London Road (A40), Lewknor, Oxfordshire OX9 5RY. (Tel: 01844 53898 Voice/Minicom)

Irish Deaf Society
30 Blessington Street, Dublin 7, Eire. (Tel: 00 353 1 8601878 Voice; 00 353 1 8601910 Minicom; Fax: 00 353 1 8601960)

LASER: The Language of Sign as an Educational Resource
c/o 8 Church Lane, Kimpton, Hitchen, Hertfordshire SG4 8RP. (Tel: 01438 832676 Voice and Text, Fax: 01438 833699)

National Association of Deafened People
Longacre, Horsleys Green, High Wycombe, Buckinghamshire HP14 3UX.

The National Deaf Children's Society
National Office 15 Dufferin Street, London EC1Y 8PD (Tel: 0171-250 0123 Voice and Text, Parents' Helpline 2pm - 5pm 0800 252380; Fax: 0171 2515020)

'Read Hear'
PO Box 701, Glasgow G42 9XG. (Tel: 0141-632 0024 Voice / Fax 0141-649 0597 Text)

The Royal National Institute for Deaf People
19-23 Featherstone Street, London EC1Y 8SL (Tel: 0171-296 8000 Voice, 0171-296 8001 Text; Fax: 0171-296 8199)

Scottish Association of Sign Language Interpreters (SASLI)
31 York Place, Edinburgh EH1 3HP. (Tel: 0131-557 6370 Voice and Text; Fax: 0131-557 4110)

Sense: The National Deaf-Blind and Rubella Association
11-13 Clifton Terrace, Finsbury Park, London N4 3SR. (Tel: 0171–272 7774 Voice and Qwerty)

Sound Advantage plc
1 Metro Centre, Werbeck Way, Peterborough PE2 7UH. (Tel: 01733 361199. Text 01733 238020)

TYPETALK: National Telephone Relay Service
Pauline Ashley House, Ravenside Retail Park, Speke, Liverpool L24 8QB. (Tel: 0151–494 1000 general enquiries. Freephone 0800 500888 Registration, Text only)

United Kingdom Council on Deafness
PO Box 13, Abbots Langley, Hertfordshire WD5 0RQ. (Tel: 01923 264584 Voice/ Minicom)

Wales Council for the Deaf
Glen View House, Coathouse Street, Pontypridd, Wales CF37 1JW.
(Tel: 01443 485687 / 485686 Voice/Minicom; Fax: 01443 408555)

SOURCES AND RECOMMENDED READING

BOOKS

BRENNAN, M., COLVILLE, M. and LAWSON, L. (1980). *Words in Hand: A structural analysis of the signs of British Sign Language*. Edinburgh: Moray House College of Further Education.

CONRAD, R. (1979). *The Deaf Schoolchild: Language and Cognitive Function*. London: Harper & Row.

EVANS, L. (1982). *Total Communication: Structure and Strategy*. Washington DC: Gallaudet College Press.

FLETCHER, L. (1987). *Language for Ben: A deaf child's right to sign*. London: Souvenir Press.

FRISHBERG, N. (1985). *Interpreting: An introduction*. Textbooks in Interpretation.

GREGORY, S. and HARTLEY, G. (1991). *Constructing Deafness*. Pinter Publishers in association with the Open University.

HEBDIGE, D. (1979). *Subculture: The meaning of style*. London: Methuen & Co. Ltd.

JACKSON, P. (1990). *Britain's Deaf Heritage*. Edinburgh: The Pentland Press Limited.

KLIMA, E. and BELLUGI, U. (1979). *The Signs of Language*. Harvard University Press.

KYLE, J. G. and WOLL, B. (1985). *Sign Language: The study of deaf people and their language*. Cambridge University Press.

LANE, H. (1987). *When the Mind Hears: A history of the deaf*. London: Souvenir Press.

MILES, D. (1988). *British Sign Language: A beginner's guide*. London: BBC Books.

OPEN UNIVERSITY D251 (1991). *Issues in Deafness. Course Units*. Milton Keynes: The Open University.

Unit 1: *Perspectives on Deafness: An introduction*. Prepared for the course team by George Taylor and Susan Gregory.

Unit 2: *The Deaf Community*. Prepared for the course team by Jim Kyle.

Unit 3: *British Sign Language, Communication and Deafness*. Prepared for the course team by Susan Gregory and Dorothy Miles.

PADDEN, C., and HUMPHRIES, T. (1988). *Deaf in America: Voices from a culture*. Harvard University Press.

QUIGLEY, S. P. and PAUL, P. V. (1984). *Language and Deafness*. California: College-Hill Press.

ROBINSON, K. (1991). *Children of Silence*. London: Penguin Books.

SACKS, O. (1990). *Seeing Voices: A journey into the world of the deaf*. London: Pan Books Ltd.

SMITH, C. (1988). *Communication Link: A dictionary of signs*. Revised edition. Middlesbrough: Beverley School for the Deaf.

SMITH, C. (1990). *Signs Make Sense: A Guide to British Sign Language*. London: Souvenir Press.

STERNBERG, M. L. A. (1987). *American Sign Language Dictionary*. New York: Harper & Row.

TAYLOR, G. and GREGORY, S. (1991). *Being Deaf: the experience of deafness*. Pinter Publishers in association with the Open University.

WOLL, B., KYLE, J. and DEUCHAR, M. (1981). *Perspectives on British Sign Language and Deafness*. London: Croom Helm.

VIDEOS

British Sign Language: A beginner's guide. BBC Video, PO Box 100, Nailsea, Bristol BS19 1AM.

Sign 1–10: An Introduction to British Sign Language (BSL). Moray House College of Further Education, Holyrood Road, Edinburgh EH8 8AQ.

Video materials are also available to students of BSL through the Council for the Advancement of Communication with Deaf People (CACDP), Pelaw House, School of Education, University of Durham, Durham City DH1 1TA.

PERIODICALS

The British Deaf News. Published monthly. Journal of the British Deaf Association, 1–3 Worship Street, London EC2A 2AB.

Hearing Concern. Published quarterly. Journal of Hearing Concern: the British Association of the Hard of Hearing, 7–11 Armstrong Road, London W3 7JL.

See Hear! Published monthly. The Royal National Institute for Deaf People in association with BBC Education.

Talk. Published quarterly. Journal of the National Deaf Children's Society, 15 Dufferin Street, London EC1Y 8PD.

Talking Sense. Published quarterly. SENSE: The National Deaf-Blind and Rubella Association, 11–13 Clifton Terrace, Finsbury Park, London N4 3SR.

INFORMATION BOOKLETS

LISTENING EYE. Tyne Tees Television production for Channel 4. (1990). *Signs of Our Times.*
LISTENING EYE. Tyne Tees Television production for Channel 4. (1991). *Looking to the Future.*
ROCHESTER INSTITUTE OF TECHNOLOGY. *Tips for Communication with Deaf People.* Rochester: New York.

INFORMATION PACKS/LEAFLETS

British Telecom's Guide to Equipment and Services for Disabled Customers 1991.
The British Deaf Association Information Pack.
The Council for the Advancement of Communication with Deaf People Information Pack.
Deaf Accord: A Consortium of Deaf Consumer Organisations Information Leaflet.
LASER: Language of Sign as an Educational Resource Information Leaflet.
The National Deaf Children's Society Information Pack.
The Royal National Institute for Deaf People Information Pack.
SENSE: The National Deaf-Blind and Rubella Association Information Pack.

ARTICLES

Community Care, 26th April 1990. 'Services for Deaf People: Has Anything Changed?'
Community Care, 1st March 1990. 'Mind Your Language: Deaf Communication'.
New Scientist, 27th October 1990. 'Signs of Change'.
The British Deaf News Supplement, October 1980. 'The Renaissance of British Sign Language', by Mary Brennan and Allan B. Hayhurst.

TELEVISION PROGRAMMES AND TELETEXT INFORMATION SERVICES

BBC Television 'See Hear!'
Tyne Tees Television for Channel 4 'Sign On'.
BBC Television 'Read Hear'.
Channel 4 'Deafview'.